IMPACT

IMPACT

THE HUMAN STORIES BEHIND IRELAND'S ROAD TRAGEDIES

Jenny McCudden

The Collins Press

FIRST PUBLISHED IN 2010 BY
The Collins Press
West Link Park
Doughcloyne
Wilton
Cork

British Library Cataloguing in Publication Data
McCudden, Jenny.
    Impact : the human stories behind Ireland's road
tragedies.
    1. Traffic accidents--Ireland. 2. Traffic accident
victims--Ireland--Interviews.
    I. Title
363.1'25'09417-dc22
ISBN-13: 9781848890275

Typesetting by The Collins Press
Typeset in Goudy and Trajan
Printed in Great Britain by J F Print Ltd

Cover photographs
Front: © iStockphoto.com
Back: © iStockphoto.com/caracterdesign.
Author photo on pg i: Andrew Downes

CONTENTS

FOREWORD

This is a different kind of road safety message. It will shock, but because of the sensitive tone, readers will not have to look away, tune out or close the book. In fact, they will find this book hard to put down, for the simple reason that they will care about the people inside it. *Impact* takes statistics and turns them into real-life stories. This is not a snapshot of lost lives, but rather a fitting tribute to the victims of road crashes and their families. These people have opened their hearts and the rawness of their grief so that this book could be written. Their resilience is commendable; their courage can only be admired. So many families are living the nightmare: they've heard the knock in the middle of the night, seen the telltale yellow jackets on the other side of the windowpane, screamed out to nothing but silence. For the people who love them, a person can never be a mere statistic, a faceless name, a number. Jenny McCudden's book reminds us of this precious fact. It also highlights our vulnerability as road users, another truth that is so often overlooked. No one ever thinks it is going to happen to them – until it does. Hundreds of people die on Irish roads every year, thousands more are injured. Lives are totally destroyed. The reality of living with a brain or spinal injury is laid bare within these pages. A young executive from a top mobile phone company learns how to switch on a computer by himself, his feat for the day. The same man once travelled the globe as part of his job. A solicitor who crashed on the way to her wedding-dress fitting will now never walk up the aisle. There are so many tragic circumstances to consider when it comes to the aftermath of road crashes. *Impact* offers an understanding of what it means when lives are shattered within seconds, because, behind the wheel, every second counts.

Gay Byrne
January 2010

INTRODUCTION

A Quiet Catastrophe

The crash scene has been cleared, but the signs of death are everywhere. The road is wide and straight. Summer sunlight bakes the tarmac so that it looks as if it is melting, the surface like ripples in a stream. We arrive, as always, after the event and search for clues. Tyre tracks, a hole in the wall, a passport photo from a driver's licence. I wonder if I have become immune to the tragedy that is a road death when I call my cameraman to take a shot of a bunch of fresh flowers.

I stoop down to a child's line of vision to read the sympathy note, looking for a poignant line, a word or expression that encapsulates the grief of a loved one left behind. Perched among the pink carnations, under the rain-drenched plastic, and scrawled in lazy handwriting is the message: *Luv ya and miss ya forever buddy, won't forget ya.*

A car pulls into the hard shoulder and a middle-aged man in a black shirt gets out, slamming the door shut.

Instinctively I know this man has just lost his son, a fact later confirmed by a local resident. He is studying the road, wanting to see it with his own eyes, seeking some sort of explanation. His hands act as a sun visor as he peers into the distance. Taking a number of long strides from the skid marks to the damaged wall, he counts in his head, trying to make sense of the senseless. An arrow of swallows swoops past, twittering in the quiet. The man hears nothing but the voice of his teenage son. He reads the sympathy messages; they take his breath away. With his right hand clasped to his mouth, he leaves.

From a discreet distance, we capture his image as he walks slowly away, the picture of anguish. Later that day, this broken man will be shown on the TV3 News bulletin, along with a smiling photo of his dead son, taken from Bebo.

News stories follow a formula. Road deaths are tragic and the tone of any report should reflect that tragedy in a sensitive manner. We talk to the gardaí, the emergency services, the local parish priest and the neighbours who come out to help when they hear the loud noise in the middle of the night. We try to piece together what went wrong with the facts that we have been given. We make no judgements. I realise as I edit the report that I have covered too many of these stories, seen too many smashed-up vehicles, twisted pieces of metal, a collection of obscene modern sculptures, hidden at the back of Garda stations: the proof of lives wasted.

Multiple fatalities happen all too frequently. Young men and women with the world at their feet never think that life could end for them, so they take risks, insane chances. I know because I took them myself without ever considering the consequences. As a teenager I accepted lifts home from rural discos with drunk drivers. Perched on someone's knee, no seat belts, music blaring, cigarette smoke blinding us, we drove home, the car journey sometimes as much fun as the nightclub itself. This was excitement. This was the 1990s. Driving laws were not so strict, attitudes less stringent. We would not get caught. We could trust the driver – he was good-looking and smart. The fact that he had been drinking pints of beer all night was overlooked because it was not an issue. His inebriated state did not even feature on my radar.

It is for this reason, in particular, that I took on this project. Because I want to let every teenager know that I was one of the fortunate ones. I considered myself sensible, always bright, sharp, ambitious, friendly; rarely foolish. I was blind to the dangers of drink-driving, of speeding along in an overcrowded car full of raucous teens. When I think back now at the road safety risks I took, my mature mind can hardly take it in. Not only do I shudder and cringe, I thank my lucky stars that I have lived to tell the tale.

I am not implying that I am indicative of every teenager, but I believe that I shared many of the same traits as teenagers of this generation: the carefree, idealistic, it-won't-happen-to-me attitude. But I know now that it can, and does. As Western Correspondent for TV3 News, I see it first hand, the groups of friends huddled together outside funeral homes. I notice the hallmarks of youth, streaked blonde hair, Converse runners, school uniforms, and tears, so many tear-stained cheeks. This is what real disbelief feels like – not the 'I don't believe I will crash' type, but the 'I can't believe he is dead' kind.

A road statistic is something we should all strive never to become. My first cousin was twenty-one years old when he was killed in a road traffic collision on a cold January evening in 2003. He was not speeding, just unlucky. Leaving the M50 toll bridge plaza, an articulated truck hit his motorbike. He died instantly. This blond boy, as a smiling, cheeky child, played chasing in my parents' back garden, and ran through golden meadows next to my grandmother's house in County Mayo, bounding over hills, captured in photos and in my mind. I didn't really know him as an adult, but those who did speak of his beautiful spirit and kind nature.

I write this book knowing that most families in Ireland have some experience of the heartache of road crashes, the infinite void that an instant can leave. This book is for them, for those who have to live with the consequences of yesterday's news.

From Letterkenny to Limerick, I cover stories along the western seaboard. The locations may vary but there is nowhere in my patch untouched by road deaths. I don't report on every fatal crash, because there are too many. I fear that the public sometimes switch off from the shocking statistics of deaths and serious injuries on our roads, that such tragedy continues on as a quiet catastrophe, lost somewhere in the running order of life. This book takes statistics and turns them into real-life stories, because only then do they become relevant in the fight against road carnage.

People make things real: not some abstract figure we must improve on, but the sounds of crying children trapped in the back seat, the dazed driver on side of the road, the initial silence after a head-on smash. I heard that silence

4

once and will never forget how strange it sounded. We were en route to a news story in County Clare. The cameraman, Oisín Moran, was driving while I scribbled into my notebook in the passenger seat. Joe Duffy was pontificating in an endearing tone, as only he can. The mid-afternoon sunlight was glorious. It was July 2009 and summer had finally arrived. I glanced up at the magnificent vista. A purple haze illumined the distance bogs; velvet green hills looked ripe for picnics.

As we approached the brow of a hill, a cloud of ominous black smoke drifted into the piercingly blue sky. 'Jesus!' Oisín said, and I knew something was very wrong. The traffic had come to a halt. There were three cars in front of us, before the gap in the road, where the smoke now billowed up. 'What happened?' I asked as we, like the vehicles in front of us, pulled into the hard shoulder. It then became clear that there had just been a head-on collision. One car was in the middle of the road, facing the wrong way; the other had smashed into the ditch on the opposite side of the single-carriageway. Drivers abandoned cars, some running, others walking cautiously towards the crashed cars and the unfortunate people inside them. I followed the small knot of people, but I needed reassurance that I was doing the right thing. In those initial moments, the silence of the unspoken was astounding. It was like a scene from a post-apocalyptic movie, stunned civilians in slow motion. And it hit me then that it is always civilians who first come across scenes like this; ordinary people with no training trying to help.

I called the emergency services. So did everyone else. We approached the car in the ditch with another man who shouted for some tools. Oisín found a spanner in the back of the jeep and offered it up. 'I think he's trying to manoeuvre the smashed bonnet to turn off the engine,' he said. I was no longer listening because I could see that the driver of the car in the ditch was dead. His head was halfway through the front windscreen. He was as lifeless as a child's soft toy. The nausea was instantaneous, no warning. I vomited into the long grass beside the barbed wire. I could hear the sound of children screaming, coming from the other car. My shock rendered me useless. Here was I, a journalist, having researched road deaths for the past two months, getting sick on the side of the road. Fighting back tears, I wanted to be anywhere but where I was. Fortunately, some of the people on the scene came from a medical background. They told me to find towels, but to stay back. 'Is there anything I can do?' I inquired again. 'No, just stay back, please. Thanks.' The emergency services arrived and the road was closed off. I felt privileged to witness their ability to place order on a chaotic situation. Taking a detour, we drove home, talking non-stop, as if by talking we, too, could place some order on our chaotic thoughts.

Reporting on road deaths is difficult. This book has been emotionally draining to write but if it helps to save even one life, then it will have been worth it all. Nine out of ten collisions on Irish roads are the result of driver error, the over-confident young man, the over-the-limit executive, the mother with screaming kids in the back, the inexperienced girl who checks her lipstick once too often, the long-distance truck driver who gives in to sleep, the split-second lapse in concentration which can have catastrophic consequences.

INTRODUCTION

Individual drivers can make a difference. All it takes are small changes. My hope is that this book may help you to do that.

1

CARNAGE ON THE M50

'One day I probably will fall apart, but not now.' Lindsey Cawley

When the doorbell rang on Sunday morning, 23 November 2004, Lindsey Cawley was not expecting visitors. The nineteen-year-old covered her ears with her manicured hands. *Go away*, she groaned under her breath, still in the throes of the stomach upset that had kept her at home. The painkillers had not yet kicked in. Earlier, Lindsey, who was planning to go shopping with her family, had opted instead to stay in bed. Traipsing through the bustling streets of eager shoppers would have taken stamina. Lengthy queues, screaming children and loud, gum-chewing teens did not appeal to her. She had already been feeling queasy enough with an upset stomach. A hassle-free day was what she needed, with time to rest.

She stretched under the duvet, willing the uninvited guests to go away. The shrill sound of the doorbell persisted. Lindsey pulled on a tracksuit and made her way downstairs. She rubbed her eyes before focusing on the front door. It was then she noticed the telltale yellow jackets through the windowpane. The two gardaí on the doorstep asked Lindsey if they could come inside. Her first thought was, 'God, what have I done?'

Lindsey was a shop assistant in the Blanchardstown Shopping Centre. She lived with her family, and kept out of trouble. What could she have done wrong? Lindsey found herself recalling her most recent nights out, delving through hazy recollections of dancing with friends or bellowing out chart-topping songs at the top of her voice. The idea that the gardaí could have been calling to report a crash did not cross her mind.

Lindsey was advised to sit down. She took a deep breath, before perching on the edge of the sofa, like a nervous interviewee. She placed her clammy hands on her knees and looked up earnestly. The garda asked her if she knew Elizabeth Cawley. 'Yes', she said, 'she's my Mam.' The garda said, 'She has been in an accident.' Lindsey imagined her mother, Betty, a clumsy woman, slipping on a café floor, tripping over her shopping bags, or falling off a curb. Her mother always made such a fuss. She probably had forgotten her mobile phone and had had to send the gardaí to let Lindsey know about her broken arm. She smiled, close-lipped, and offered an apologetic look to the gardaí. In truth, she felt slightly embarrassed. It never occurred to her that it could be something more serious.

It was. The gardaí explained that Betty had been

involved in a car crash on the M50 motorway. Lindsey was asked to accompany them to the Mater Hospital in Dublin city, where her mother was being treated. 'They never mentioned my older sister, Errin, or my younger brother, Evan, who had been in the car with my mother. It never clicked with me to ask about them.'

At the hospital, Lindsey was greeted by a nurse and taken to a family room. There, in the quiet of this small dark room, she learned for the first time the extent of her mother's injuries. 'I was told Mam was in surgery because the doctors couldn't stop the bleeding.' Lindsey asked after her siblings. Twenty-two-year-old Errin had been taken with head injuries to the Intensive Care Unit at Beaumont Hospital, while fifteen-year-old Evan was in Blanchardstown Hospital. It took just a few lines of dialogue for the improbable to become the probable, for Lindsey to realise that things that happened only to other people had suddenly happened to her.

Lindsey walked towards the front steps of the hospital. People brushed past her, some with bouquets of flowers. She tried, but couldn't make any sense of the facts. It was as if dozens of voices were speaking simultaneously. In the end, she switched off, her head empty, drained of noise. The smell of disinfectant in the corridor made her want to vomit.

Standing alone, she realised that she had neither credit nor battery power left in her mobile phone. She needed a cigarette and she rummaged around in her handbag to find only one left in the packet. Lindsey wondered what she should do. She tried to recall phone numbers in her head, but couldn't remember any. She didn't panic; she leaned against the wall and smoked. Her red nail varnish was chipped; she had been biting her nails. A frantic figure then appeared in the distance running towards her.

'A friend of mine, Sinead, had heard a report on the radio and had come to the hospital. Everyone thought it was me who was in the car crash. She ran over crying hysterically and shaking. I was telling her to calm down, saying, "it's all right, it's all right". I'm a calm person. It's the strangest thing. I was in such a daze that when I saw her, face to face, I didn't recognise who she was. I just felt I knew this person and I put my arms out to her.'

By this stage, the gardaí had also contacted Lindsey's father, Larry, who was at Beaumont Hospital with Errin, while Evan had managed to phone a family friend, who went to his bedside at Blanchardstown Hospital. A fourth passenger in the car, a fourteen-year-old friend of Evan, had been taken to Temple Street Hospital. His injuries were not life-threatening.

Lindsey waited at the Mater until she could talk to the surgeon who had operated on her mother. When he told her that Betty might not recover, Lindsey wanted to know her mother's percentage chance of survival. Her eyes locked on to his as she implored him to be as precise and honest as he could be. 'He said that all I could do was hope; all I could do was pray. We just had to wait and see.'

Forty-eight-year-old Betty Cawley, the front-seat passenger, had lost her spleen and most of her bladder in the collision. Her collarbone and breastbone were crushed. She had a large number of broken bones and ripped muscles. Lindsey was allowed to visit the post-operative room, where, under fluorescent light, Betty lay hooked up to machines. Her heartbeat flashed on a black screen, red, green and blue lines, proof that she was still alive. Nurses took notes, monitoring the squiggly patterns. The smell was unmistakably hospital bleach, the disinfectant of the sick. Nothing could have prepared Lindsey for what she now saw. 'Her shoulder was black. Her breastbone was just floating. Her arms and chest were as black as coal. She was bound really tight.' Lindsey eventually had to leave her mother, not knowing if she would survive, in order to see about her brother and sister – how badly injured were they?

Lindsey's husband, Dave, who was her boyfriend at the time, arrived at the Mater Hospital. Earlier, she had decided not to contact him, because it was his first day in a new job. It soon became clear, however, that she needed him. Her friend suggested that she call him. As soon as he heard, Dave rushed to be with Lindsey. The gardaí then escorted the couple to Blanchardstown and Beaumont Hospitals. The M50, one of the busiest stretches of road in the country, was closed for six hours that day, after the crash. Lindsey and Dave drove behind the squad car through the Phoenix Park, on the grass instead of on the congested road for most of the journey. Some frustrated motorists honked their horns at them. Lindsey focused on the flashing blue lights ahead, the even beats of the heart monitor machine still ringing in her ears. Their first stop was Blanchardstown Hospital.

Evan had suffered a broken collarbone, lacerations to the spleen, fractured ribs, a punctured lung and scarring from flying pieces of shattered glass. Hooked up to a morphine drip, Evan told Lindsey, 'Errin is dead'. 'He was convinced she was dead,' Lindsey recalls. 'He said something about her head being stuck in the steering wheel.'

Lindsey and Dave then travelled to Beaumont Hospital. Lindsey spoke with Errin's doctor, who told her that her sister had a 50 per cent chance of surviving the crash. Errin, the driver of the car, had suffered a brain injury. Before that moment, the words 'brain injury' were just words. Lindsey was about to find out what exactly they meant. 'The doctors drilled a hole in her head to relieve the pressure on Errin's brain. Her eyes were bulging because her brain was so badly swollen.' Lindsey searched for traces of her sister in the swollen, bruised face in front of her. She closed her eyes and saw Errin leaving that morning, glancing into her rear-view mirror; a twinkle in her eyes, happy.

'She was such a pretty little thing – so petite, such a girl – and to see her like that was horrendous. Her pupil had burst because of the pressure on her left eye. She was on a ventilator. Her tongue was hanging out of her mouth. She looked like a zombie.' Lindsey had to look away. It was an image that would haunt her. Errin, who was a dancer, had other injuries, including a crushed knee. As Lindsey slowly paced the room, she couldn't help thinking that her sister would probably never dance again. That night Lindsey went home to an empty house. The three people she lived with were lying in separate hospitals across north Dublin.

The day had begun like any other Sunday in the Cawley household. Larry and Betty Cawley had been separated for a number of years. The children remained close to their father, but they lived with Betty in their Blanchardstown home. The smell of a cooked breakfast lingered in the air downstairs. Betty was deciding what to wear, sifting through clothes in her wardrobe, before going shopping with her two daughters in Grafton Street.

It was a month to Christmas and already seasonal lights were draped above the city centre streets. People would be walking about with a festive step, lighter than usual. Betty chose her outfit. She loved this time of year. High-pitched noises came from Evan's room. He was practising his martial arts movements in preparation for a class later that day. At just fifteen, he was enjoying the challenge of his latest hobby. Lindsey, who was still in bed, had begun to feel unwell. She changed her mind about going shopping.

Outside, Errin honked the horn of her new Nissan Almera. It had not been easy, but the determined young driver had passed her driving test. The next step was to invest in a set of wheels, and after saving up the cash, she splashed out on the car. 'She loved that car,' says Lindsey, 'it was her baby. She'd only had it a few weeks when the crash happened.'

A youth worker in the local community, Errin taught dance and ran a homework club. She was also employed part-time in the Blanchardstown Shopping Centre. 'Errin was the Cawley cab, always happy to drop us wherever we needed to go,' Lindsey explains. 'She was a cautious driver, who adhered to the speed limit and insisted that all her passengers wear seat belts.'

As she switched on the ignition, Errin turned to her brother and his friend in the back seat, making sure that they fastened their seat belts. She had agreed to drop the boys to their martial arts class at the nearby Dublin City University. Betty Cawley sat in to the passenger seat, looking forward to a day's shopping with her daughter. Smiling, she flicked the fir-shaped air freshener. Lindsey waved goodbye to her family before going back to bed.

The car pulled out of the Brookhaven estate, situated close to the Blanchardstown Shopping Centre, and drove towards the motorway. The journey took less than ten minutes. As usual, the M50 was busy with weekend traffic. Errin was driving in the inside lane, but moved into the outside lane to make way for other motorists who were about to join the motorway from the slip road at Finglas. She was now driving northbound next to the grass median that separated the two sides of the motorway. (At that time, there was no crash barrier along that section of the road, but one has since been erected.)

At the same time, a 27-year-old Latvian man was travelling in the opposite direction, southbound. Pavels Desjatnikovs, who lived in Lucan, was driving erratically, overtaking on the inside lane. He was also driving with no insurance. A number of witnesses reported him later for dangerous driving. Moments before the crash, one driver called a traffic watchdog number to report him. The calls could not prevent what happened next. Pavels Desjatnikovs lost control of his car. It crossed the grass verge and somersaulted through the air before landing on the bonnet of Errin Cawley's car.

Evan Cawley, in the back seat, was looking out of the side window. He did not see the car hurtling towards them. The teenager, who is now nineteen, remembers his mother's reaction: 'I'll never forget her screams. That's the first thing I recall about the crash.' Evan says that the moment of impact was so sudden that he finds it difficult to put into words. He is unsure if he can even remember it. He just knows that, within a few seconds, he was splattered with blood. 'I got up slowly from the back seat and climbed out of the car. I carried my friend out of the car. He asked me to lift up his top and I saw blood all over his stomach. I was crippled over with a really bad pain.'

Evan then did something that can be explained only by shock: the fifteen-year-old started to walk down the hard shoulder of the M50 on his own, without turning back. He had nowhere to go, but he kept walking for about five minutes before picking a spot on the side of the road and sitting down. Putting his bloody hands up to his face, he started to sob. 'It then hit me, all of a sudden, that Mam and Errin were still in the car. I went back to see if they were all right. Mam was sitting in the front seat with her eyes staring straight ahead in a kind of daze; they were wide open but she couldn't say anything. I said to her a few times, "Mam, are you all right?" She just sat there looking so angry. It was as if she was trying to say something to me in her head, but no words came out.' Another image that will never leave Evan is that of the gospel choir who happened to be travelling northbound in a minibus when the crash happened. The group stood on the tarmac, singing hymns softly, while waiting for the emergency services to arrive. Evan thought later this was a dream.

Betty Cawley used to wonder how any of them got out alive. 'It will always be crystal clear in my head. The image of that car somersaulting through the sky; it was just so unbelievable. The things I remember are the silence after it happened, the strong smell of burning rubber and metal and my daughter Errin's head on my shoulder.'

Errin Cawley's memory of that day will never be

known. Less than a week after the crash, on 4 December 2004, she died in Beaumont Hospital.

In the days following the crash, Lindsey divided her time between the three hospitals, hoping and praying that Errin and Betty would pull through. One day the hospital told her that Errin's brain had died. 'I had to wait for forty minutes before I could see her while they took all the tubes out of her.' What Lindsey saw was frightening. 'Her tongue was still hanging out of her mouth; she was completely bloated, her bulging eyes had not closed. Blood leaked from her ears and nose. It was something nobody should ever have to see – someone you love lying dead like that.' Lindsey felt a wave of fear wash over her; her teeth chattered and she could taste bile at the back of her throat. 'It's very strange to be scared of somebody you love, but I couldn't help it.'

Lindsey felt an immense loneliness, as if all the important things about her had disappeared – Errin was not just her sister, but a best friend, the one who knew all her secrets. Errin helped make sense of Lindsey's life. Without her, how would she cope? In whom would she confide? Lindsey wanted to see her mother. She made her way to the Mater Hospital, where Betty lay unconscious, fighting for her life. Betty could not talk to Lindsey. She could not stroke her forehead or tell her everything was going to be all right. There were no words of comfort; there were no words at all.

'What do you do when everything goes wrong? You go straight to your Mam,' she says. 'Errin was gone and I just needed to be beside my mother.'

Lindsey recorded Errin's funeral on video, so that her mother, if she survived, would be able to see it. 'To grieve properly, Mam would need to see Errin lying in her coffin and the coffin going into the ground. Otherwise, it wouldn't have been real to her. You can't grieve for somebody you haven't lost.'

Evan was allowed out of hospital for the funeral at St Patrick's Church in Blanchardstown. Hundreds gathered there to pay their respects. It was a very painful day for the Cawley family. 'I looked around the church at this sea of people and was so proud of her,' says Lindsey. On her sixteenth birthday, Errin had bought Lindsey a poem about sisters, printed in calligraphy on a scroll. From the altar, Lindsey read the verse, and it was only at the close that she wept.

As Errin was being buried, Betty began to regain consciousness. For the first few days and weeks, everything was confusing. Having no recollection of the crash, she believed she was in hospital for another reason. 'I have cancer, don't I? I'm dying of cancer,' she said.

Lindsey got into a routine, spending full days at the hospital to help take care of her mother. 'I would rub cream on to her legs and we would chat about trivial things.' She decided not to mention the crash, believing that Betty would talk about it when she was ready to face up to what had happened. The last thing Lindsey wanted was having to tell her twice. 'Rushing her would have been the wrong thing to do. I was not prepared to tell her about Errin's death until I was certain she could understand.'

A few days later, as Lindsey was massaging her mother's feet, Betty inquired after Errin. 'Where's Errin? Are the two of you fighting again?' she said, before asking, 'Why do the two of you keep coming in separately? The two of you are fighting, aren't you?' 'Mam was convinced that she was seeing this pink blur between falling asleep and waking up,' Lindsey says. 'Errin always wore pink. We used to call her the Pink Lady. Mam presumed it was Errin, but it was me because from the day Errin died, I have always worn a piece of pink clothing.'

Lindsey kept gently working the cream into her mother's skin, refusing to make eye contact with her. But one day Betty started to talk about the crash. Her questions became more specific, her tone more urgent. She wanted to know where Errin was being treated. Slowly a picture began to take shape in her head: an oncoming car, a collision, horror. Betty persisted, 'Where's Errin? Where's Errin?' Lindsey finally said, 'Errin didn't make it.' Betty was stunned, but said 'Okay.' She had no other words. For ten minutes, they sat in silence.

Three months after the crash, Betty's feeding tubes were removed and she was permitted to spend a short time away from the hospital on day leave. She watched the funeral of her dead daughter for the first time. Then she watched it again, and again. Lindsey began to worry. 'Seeing the funeral helped her, but we should have destroyed the tape after she had watched it once.' Lindsey had to coax the video away from her mother, as if she were a toddler with an unsuitable toy.

After three months Betty Cawley was eventually discharged from the Mater, but her quality of life would never be the same again. She needed help to dress; she had to be bathed by others. She also suffered from fibromyalgia, a condition characterised by chronic pain in the muscles, joints and soft tissue, and by fatigue. She woke up feeling exhausted, weak and in pain. Because she had lost most of her bowel in the crash, she had to visit the bathroom about thirty times a day. She was effectively housebound. In any case, Betty no longer had the inclination to go anywhere. Besides her physical ailments, she was depressed.

'It was very hard for Mam. She used to say "I can't go on with this life". She spent weeks in bed when she first came home from the hospital. Evan and I would have to go upstairs and plead with her to get up. Sometimes we had to climb in beside her until she got so irritated that she would finally get up and come downstairs. I looked after my mother for such a long time. It was like the roles were reversed. I saw her as my baby. I was so protective over her. No one could take her out unless they got instructions from me as to what she could eat. I was the only person who knew what tablets she had to take, because I dispensed them.'

Betty was fearful of driving. It would be two years before she would get behind the wheel of a car. The family got into a daily routine, coaxing Betty out from the front porch to the car. Some days she would simply walk slowly around the vehicle, stalking it like prey. On other days, she would progress to sitting into the passenger seat. She would fasten her seat belt, then immediately regret the decision and get out of the car. Betty would sometimes manage to sit in the car for a full five minutes with both doors closed – a feat in itself. She would then go back into the house, her good deed done for the day. 'We nearly had to sedate her when it was time to drive to the hospital,' Lindsey says.

But, against all odds, Betty overcame her fear of cars and of the open road. Lindsey wonders how her mother ever smiled again, considering that her days were mapped out by medication and frequent trips to the bathroom. 'The amount of tablets Mam had to take put immense strain on her liver. She would get moments when she honestly believed she would have been better off dead, but there were also those times when things started to look up for her.'

In 2006, Lindsey and Dave had a baby girl, Ruby, who brought much-needed joy to the Cawley family, giving Betty, in particular, a new reason for living. Before the birth of her granddaughter, Betty was steeped in depression. She would spend hours in her room weeping, rocking on her bed, wallowing in a world she despised. Her red-rimmed eyes held no hope. Ruby changed that. Betty began to look forward to the future.

In the first few weeks, Betty was there through the many sleepless nights to help Lindsey and offer advice. 'She adored Ruby and wanted to be with her all the time. When Ruby was a month old, Mam took her for a walk around the block. She couldn't walk very far, but she would try her best; she was the proudest grandmother in Blanchardstown. I have a playroom packed to capacity with toys, all from Mam.'

Betty had been a generous person, and not just with her own family. The door of her home in Brookhaven Close was always open. Betty could be seen bent over her sewing machine, with colourful materials strewn across the dining-room table, as she made costumes for the local theatre group. She would voluntarily devote her time to making costumes and supervising rehearsals. Helping others was second nature to this spirited Dublin woman, who always used her talents for the benefit of the community. Her family say it is hardly surprising that she became a road safety campaigner. Despite her poor health, in 2007 Betty took part in a television advertisement on behalf of the Road Safety Authority, becoming a public voice for families who had been bereaved by road deaths.

In August 2008 Betty was at Lindsey's wedding. Like most brides, Lindsey was flustered before her big day. In her bedroom, she tried on her white dress, twirled in front of the full-length mirror twenty times and still couldn't see what she had liked so much in the shop. She attempted to hide her disappointment, but her wide smile did not reach her eyes. Smoothing the skirt down one last time, she sighed. Betty sat silently on the edge of the bed.

'You're coming with me,' she told Lindsey. They took a taxi to an exclusive bridal shop in the city centre, where Lindsey found her fairytale wedding dress. The cost was €2,000. Betty paid the bill. The grand gesture was to be one of the last Betty made for her daughter. Her health was deteriorating rapidly, an affliction she bore with dignity, choosing not to complain, but rather to take in her stride. She tried not to let it get her down, but it was not always possible for her to stay positive.

On the day of the wedding, Betty was particularly weak. She tried to keep a low profile, believing that this would be better for her daughter. So when Lindsey slid into her expensive gown, Betty was not there to help her, and when she walked down the stairs, her mother was not waiting in the hallway with a camera. Later, at the reception, Betty retired to her hotel room for much of the day.

'Everyone has this image of their mother turning to them on their wedding day to tell them they look beautiful. My Mam wore a blank look. She was really sick with end-stage liver disease, dealing with the pain and exhaustion of it, all on her own. None of us knew how ill she really was at the time. Now I know that she was staying out of the way, concealing her pain, for me on my big day.'

Four months later, on 13 December 2008, Betty Cawley died as a result of complications linked to injuries sustained in the M50 crash. She spent the last few weeks of her life back in the Mater Hospital, where she was a much-loved, popular patient to the end.

'Mam died at 10.45 in the morning,' Lindsey says. 'I had just fallen asleep. One of the nurses cleared me a space on the bed, so I could lie down beside her. My head was next to hers. We all then left the room for a few minutes. Betty waited until we'd left the room and then she died. She had faded away to nothing. Seconds after she died, my mother looked like a different person. Her skin was very yellow; her hands were puffed up. It was a fight until the bitter end; that was the story of her life. This woman never gave up. In the end, she was in a coma, but she was still alive to me. When someone is alive, you don't care if they're asleep; you just want them there. It's clutching at straws, but it's just the way the brain works, you want them there and you don't care what way they are; you just want them there.'

It was close to Christmas, her mother's favourite time. Every year, she bought more decorations to add to her ever-expanding collection. Twelve overflowing boxes, packed with glittering tinsel and fairy lights, were already stored in the attic. Betty had plans to get her Christmas shopping done, telling the family, 'I know I can't walk very far, but I don't care if I have to do my Christmas shopping in a wheelchair. If this is my last Christmas, I'm doing my Christmas shopping.'

Evan's teenage friends helped him carry her coffin. None of them could hold back the tears. 'I know when people die, we tend to put them on a pedestal. That irritates me, but I cannot find a flaw in her because she did what she could for everybody, to the best of her ability. She was a very courageous woman.' Lindsey says Errin was quite similar to Betty.

'Both were into drama, showbiz and working with children. Errin would have got that from my mother. She was the Pink Lady, always very bubbly.'

At twenty-three, Lindsey has organised the funerals of her sister and her mother. It is December 2008, just two weeks after Betty's funeral. Pregnant with her second child, this attractive, smiling young woman is hopeful for the future. Recently Lindsey dyed her hair tomato-red, a funky look that she wears well. She shares her home with her husband, Dave, and Ruby, now two. Evan also stays in the house. The family live in Brookhaven Close in Blanchardstown, a few doors down from the house where Lindsey was reared, and a short distance from the M50, the road that claimed the lives of the two people she was closest to in the world. A shrine sits on the sideboard in her cosy sitting room: framed photographs of Errin and Betty fight for space on the pinewood top.

Lindsey often wonders about the man who drove the car that smashed into her family. She questions why he was driving with no insurance. Since he had little experience of driving on Irish roads, she doubts that he would have passed an Irish driving test.

'Errin had no time to react. Maybe they drive more erratically in Latvia. Maybe it's part of their culture. My sister was abiding by the rules of the road, in her country, where she had successfully passed her driving test. She was on the right side of the road. She did not deserve to die like that.'

Lindsey believes that, if you commit a crime, you should serve the time and is disappointed that, on 1 May 2007, Pavels Desjatnikovs was given a four-month sentence after admitting to charges of dangerous driving and driving without insurance. A number of witnesses came forward to describe how he had driven dangerously on the morning of the crash. The Director of Public Prosecutions directed that Desjatnikovs should face a simple charge of dangerous driving after an engineer's report had suggested that there was a difficulty with the brakes of his car. He was disqualified from driving for twelve months.

In court, Lindsey met Desjatnikovs face to face. 'He stood there looking at me. He damaged the tear duct of one eye in the crash, so he is continually weeping down one side of his face. He said his heart had a stone in it and he thought about Errin every day. All he wanted was my forgiveness, but I shook my head and said "No".'

2

THE PAIN OF KINSALE

'We need a miracle to get out of this one.' Batt Coleman

It was the last Sunday in September 2001 and the chill of the changing seasons had crept into the air. Batt Coleman, a 57-year-old publican, woke unusually early at 6 a.m., and then did something that was out of character: he checked his son's bedroom. Two days earlier, fifteen-year-old Conor had returned home for the weekend from boarding school in Fermoy, County Cork. He had mentioned to Batt that he was going to see a film the night before. His bedroom was empty, the curtains open, and his bed had not been slept in. Arsenal posters were pinned to the wall, a school blazer hung on the back of a chair. As Batt picked up a Cork GAA bag from the bed, he wondered was there such a thing as men's intuition. Where on earth could Conor be? He was not allowed to stay out all night. Why did he not call? Batt cursed his son under his breath before checking the rest of the house.

The family lived above the Fields pub in Dunderrow, near Kinsale, County Cork. Batt checked the front bar. The air was stagnant with the smell of stale beer. He picked up a few empty pint glasses from the bar counter and put them in the sink, then walked outside. It had rained for much of the previous day and the winding roads were still damp. The pub stood silent and alone at the small country crossroads. Batt heard the early morning crows in the distance and shivered.

Angry, he paced the bar once or twice before waking his wife, Mary. She picked up her mobile phone from the bedside locker. Batt knew that wherever Conor was, he was asleep. 'For goodness sake,' he said, 'will you put that away. He's not really going to answer the phone at this hour of the morning for you to give out to him.'

Batt and Mary knew that Conor had gone out the night before with his best friends, fifteen-year-old twins Cian and Gavin O'Sullivan, as well as 22-year-old Paul O'Donovan. The three teenagers looked up to Paul because he worked for Budget Car Hire at Cork Airport and he had a car.

The couple decided to wake up their youngest son, fourteen-year-old Gavin, who told them he had taken a call from Conor at about 9.25 p.m. the previous night. 'You'll never guess where I am,' Conor had boasted. He was calling to tell him he was having the time of his life, sitting in the back of a fast car, enjoying the ride.

Batt found himself going over these details. He saw no cause for alarm. Conor must be in the twins' house, he thought. Mary served a pot of tea. Gavin sat at the table. His face was anxious and he kept biting his lower lip. The family then started to make calls. Mary called the O'Sullivan house, only to discover that the twins too were missing.

Both families grew more concerned. News of a fatal collision in Ballinhassig, close to Kinsale, had reached the village of Dunderrow, but it was understood that the crash victims were foreign nationals.

Gavin Coleman then called Paul O'Donovan's house. Paul's mother answered, complaining that it was early in the morning and that he should call back later. Gavin persisted. She reluctantly went to wake up her son. Moments later, she came back to the phone. Paul had not come home either.

By this stage, shortly before 8 a.m., the speculation in the O'Sullivan household was that the crash had involved their twins. 'My wife had been speaking to Ann O'Sullivan,' Batt recalls, 'whom she described as being hysterical. The word was they were all dead. So I called Ann myself, and told her to stop being ridiculous. She then gave me the number of Bandon Garda Station and told me to ring them for myself.'

Batt's mind was racing as he dialled the number, his fingers unsteady. What would he do if he found out his son was dead? He was afraid he might fall apart, forget how to breathe. Images of Conor flashed in front of his eyes. He saw him shouting at the soccer screen, hitting a hurl on the lawn outside, eating buttered toast at the breakfast table – ordinary everyday things. He kept looking towards the back door. Maybe Conor would walk in with a guilty face. He would ground him for two months after this stunt. Batt could feel his chest tighten. Taking a deep breath, he told himself to dismiss hearsay; what he wanted were facts.

The phone call confirmed that Paul O'Donovan was dead. Batt needed to hear this again. Could the garda be mistaken? No. Paul was the single one of the four friends old enough to carry a driver's licence, and so the only victim who could be positively identified. Conor was fifteen, too young to carry a wallet. Mary and Gavin stared at Batt; they were trying to read the silence between his sentences. 'You have three unidentified people and we're missing three,' Batt said. He gripped the countertop, turning his face away from them. Afraid his knees would buckle under him, Batt tightened his hold. His cup of tea fell to the floor. He wanted to know what he should do next. The garda advised him to go to the hospital and to bring the twins' father, Vincent O'Sullivan, with him.

Batt made the short journey to the O'Sullivan house. The weather was grim; it was a dirty day, bleak, full of drizzle and mist. He passed a new house with children's bikes discarded on the front lawn; the grass was a posh shade of green. The countryside was washed clean. He arrived just as Vincent, who had spent the morning driving around Dunderrow looking for his sons, pulled into the driveway.

Batt looked at Vincent whose face was a mirror of his own: the stern look at the back of his eyes, the taut forehead and loose mouth. Both men knew what the other was feeling. During the 25-minute car journey to the hospital, they refused to think that their sons were dead. The car was warm, blasts of hot air keeping the windows clear. Batt turned on the radio news at 10 a.m.

'The top story concerned George Bush and Iraq, which we took as a good sign. We then tuned out, not wanting to hear any more.' As Cork University Hospital came into view, Batt turned to Vincent and said, 'We need a miracle to get out of this one.'

Batt was shown to the morgue, a place he will never forget. 'It was as big as a ballroom and there was a body, lying alone on a trolley in the middle of the room. Sure enough, it was him. His hair was sticking out, his short cropped hair with the gel still stuck to it, and not a mark on his dead face. Conor looked fine – dead, but fine.' At that moment, the instant every parent dreads, Batt would have done anything to have his son back. The only words he had were 'Oh Conor,' which he repeated quietly for the next five minutes. He looked out the window where grey skies sat like a lid on the gently sloping hills surrounding the city, and remembers hoping that there was a heaven.

Batt then phoned home to confirm the family's worst fears. He spoke to his twenty-year-old daughter Michelle. He could hear his wife Mary scream in the background, a gut-wrenching, hollow sound. Later, on the drive home, Batt wondered why he had never got to see Conor's hands. Like the rest of his body, they were covered with a white sheet.

Conor's neck snapped when the car he was travelling in lost control and crashed into an oncoming car. The collision happened at Toureen, Ballinhassig, on the main Cork to Bandon road, at 9.30 p.m., just five minutes after Conor had phoned his brother to tell him that he was having 'the time of my life'. Conor was one of six people to die in the crash; aside from the four young friends from Dunderrow who died in one car, two passengers in the other car – Denis and Nuala McCarthy, a retired couple in their sixties – were killed. The driver of that car, Declan O'Donoghue, miraculously survived. He was a nephew of Nuala McCarthy. They were driving towards their home town of Clonakilty when the crash happened. It was 29 September

2001, one of the worst weekends of carnage on Irish roads. Thirteen people were killed.

Life for the Coleman family changed irrevocably with Conor's death. Seven years later, on my visit to their home, his loss is still palpable. It's New Year's Eve 2008, and Batt serves sweet coffee and a selection of turkey and salad sandwiches, cut into triangles. The family have since moved from the Fields pub. Their new house is a granite stone bungalow, modern and stylish, with a large conservatory overlooking the countryside. There are no main roads to Dunderrow. Finding a signpost is a challenge and public transport does not pass the house: cattle do. The winding roads are narrow, bumpy and potholed, a perfect playground for young boys who enjoy driving. We talk about Conor. Batt Coleman starts to cry. He tells me about the private details of grief, the things that bothered him the most, like Conor's invisible hands. 'With most corpses, you can see the hands crossed, for example, with rosary beads. I can only imagine the mangled mess his hands must have been in.'

Framed photographs of family weddings Conor never got to attend stand on the mahogany cabinet in the corner. A fresh-faced toddler beams from another picture. The new addition to the family wears a wide smile, wisps of blond hair falling on his forehead. This was another grandchild Conor never got to meet. 'Conor will stay fifteen forever,' Batt says.

Conor was a typical teenage boy who lived for the thrills life had to offer: a gregarious lad who loved girls, football and fast cars. A sprinkling of freckles sat on the bridge of his nose and his blue eyes twinkled with his trademark cheeky grin. His dark hair was styled in spikes. Conor was the second youngest of eight children. His father looked after the pub while his mother worked in the locally based pharmaceutical factory, Eli Lilly. The Coleman family had taken the precaution of sending him to boarding school in Fermoy to keep him, as they put it, out of harm's way. 'He'd come home on a Friday, and go back on a Sunday night, and it was during that little window of opportunity that he was killed,' Batt says with a wry smile.

When Conor left the family pub that Saturday afternoon, he was in great form, happy to be home and looking forward to spending more time with his best friends, twins Cian and Gavin O'Sullivan. The trio were inseparable. They had grown up together, sharing classrooms, childhood experiences and interests, one of which, as they progressed into their teens, was fast cars. Batt was sitting in his armchair by the fireplace, catching up on the sports headlines, when he last saw Conor. 'I didn't know where he was going,' says Batt. 'We just spoke briefly about a movie he had seen or was going to see, and then he left. Mary came in from work later on and we went to bed around midnight. Conor wasn't in, but that wasn't treated too seriously. It was a weekend night and he was around the place somewhere.'

The three teenagers had taken a lift with Paul O'Donovan, who was returning a hire car to Cork Airport, but first there was some fun to be had. They drove to Kinsale where they were seen cruising around the town. They did not take the direct route to the airport; they were 'going for a burn'. 'These young fellas had no fear. They had experience of minor crashes. It didn't occur to them that they might die; that thought simply never crossed their minds,' says Batt. Despite words of warning and pleas from his parents, Conor failed to take heed. It was the same with his friends.

Ann O'Sullivan used to show her twins the papers on a Monday morning, with reports and photos of the weekend's road deaths. 'Thousands of times I warned them. Just the weekend before the crash, a young man lost his life in a single-car collision at the same spot on the road.'

Paul O'Donovan's brother, Tim, cautioned him shortly before the collision. 'I told him I didn't want to spend the rest of my life going to a cemetery to talk to him,' he says. 'But at twenty-two years of age you think you're invincible – that nothing is ever going to happen to you.'

Having formally identified their teenage sons, Batt Coleman and Vincent O'Sullivan drove home in silence. They stopped at the spot where the smash had happened. Hours earlier, the road had been cleared and reopened. The mangled wreckage of the cars had been towed away. The blood on the road had long since been washed off, and the bodies of the six people who had died on impact were now lying in the morgue.

'I looked for a sign or a signal,' says Batt, 'something to tell me what had happened, where it went wrong, but there were no answers.'

Batt then had to make the most difficult phone calls of his life. His two other sons in England had to be told that their brother was dead. The next few hours were spent on the phone, calling the extended family and friends. Batt had awoken with an uneasy feeling that Sunday morning. By lunchtime, he was meeting the local undertaker. 'I never expected that I would have to pick out a coffin for my teenage son.' The funeral home was busy. Sheets of rain fell outside. Batt was taken to a room full of coffins. He doesn't remember the different kinds of coffin, but he does remember the silk purple lining inside them. He saw the pillow where his son's head would lie. It was soft, comfortable. It would have to be comfortable, he thought.

Batt met the other anguished parents, offering whatever support he could.

'It was the first time I'd met Paul O'Donovan's mother. I think she was feeling guilty because her son was the driver.' Batt reached for her hand and pressed it gently. The families turned their attention to the logistics of arranging four funerals on the one day. Conor's parents would have to dress him one last time. What he should wear to his own funeral was another detail that had to be decided. 'He was so young, he didn't own a suit,' says Batt. 'The rest of the day is a blur; the house was constantly full. Conor was brought from the hospital to the funeral home by 4 p.m., and that was the first time Mary had seen him. There were so many people milling around outside and everyone gathered for the rosary at seven. It takes you over; you don't have time to think. I didn't eat a bite for the whole thing or take a drink. It was easier not to. Going to bed was very hard. We went upstairs around two in the morning and it was probably the first time we were alone together since it had happened. We didn't say very much. I was pacing the room, Mary was weeping. We didn't sleep. You don't sleep.'

Batt was amazed by the neighbours' generosity. People arrived with sandwiches, lasagnes, soups, homemade bread and cakes. The kettle was permanently on the boil. A continuous stream of mourners called to the house. Batt knew the community of Dunderrow was close, but it was not until the death of his son that he realised just how close. 'The phone and doorbell never stopped ringing.'

The crash attracted huge media attention; dozens of journalists came to Dunderrow to cover the funerals. Television crews hovered outside the Coleman family pub. Photographers snapped scenes from a distance. Batt was overwhelmed; he was getting tired of reporters snooping around the place. One evening, he heard an insistent knocking on the back door. He opened it to find another eager young hack with a notebook and pen at the ready. She asked him did he feel strongly about road deaths. 'It was an accident; they didn't go out there to do that. They didn't leave here to never come back,' Batt told her.

On the Monday after the collision, Batt travelled to Cork Airport to pick up his sons Stephen and Mark, who had flown home from England. The three grown men, members of a now-broken family unit, stood in Arrivals, arms locked in a communal hug. Flight announcements continued on the sound system. Passengers rushed past, pulling cases. The coffee shop was doing a steady trade. Life was going on around them, but for the Coleman family it had stopped. Batt will never forget the look on his sons' faces, their tear-rimmed eyes and quivering mouths. They looked like little boys again. Stephen and Mark usually travelled home for happy occasions, like Christmas and birthday parties, excitement intensifying with each clocked air mile. This was not a homecoming, but a heart-breaking journey.

Batt and Mary buried their son on 2 October 2001. Hundreds of mourners gathered in Kinsale for the funerals of the four friends. The coffins stood side by side in the Carmelite Friary, a small chapel in the town. The congregation sat in silence, except for the occasional distressed cry. Students in school uniforms formed guards of honour. Others followed the coffins, sobbing. It was funeral weather: bleak, dark and grey. Batt remembers throngs of distraught teenagers following the cortèges of their classmates. Conor and the twins were laid to rest in Dunderrow Cemetery, a short distance from their family homes. Paul O'Donovan was buried on that same day, as were the passengers in the other car, Nuala and Denis McCarthy.

The inquests came later but Batt Coleman did not attend. He knows every detail of how his son died. The report by the Assistant State Pathologist, Dr Margaret Bolster, found that Conor Coleman had broken arms and legs, extensive bruising and internal injuries, but the cause of death was the separation of the second and third vertebrae from the young man's spinal cord. 'It sounds so technical,' Batt says. 'That's why I always say, "What I wouldn't have done to fix it, to have put him back together again".'

Sometimes, Batt wonders if he could have done more to protect his son. 'As a parent, I examine my conscience. What could I have done – tie him down or lock him up?' He had fears that Conor's obsession with speed would get him into trouble. 'Time and again, I'd say, "Slow down, don't go driving with the older boys." Conor was not driving; he just went along for the ride.' But Batt Coleman does not attach blame.

In 2001, 418 people died on Irish roads. Conor was number 279. 'Dying in a road accident is a pretty ignominious way to die. Your life is so fragile. You have to be proactive about preserving yourself. But they got into a car. They met their death by being broken; being bumped around like rag dolls. When you're dead, you're never coming back.'

It took time, but the Coleman family have accepted that Conor is not coming home. When asked what it is they miss the most, each member of the family says the same thing – just having him around. Christmas without Conor is especially difficult. His absence is also acutely felt on happy occasions, such as a Cork All-Ireland or a family wedding.

'Two months after it happened, a friend said to me "time will improve things". I remember saying, "Don't be ridiculous, we will never get over this", and we never will, of course, but time does improve things. People say it and sometimes I don't even think they understand it themselves, but they are right – it does get better, the pain does ease. It's almost as if we're moving away and leaving him behind, but that's the facts of life. You have to.'

In 2008 the Coleman family decided not to visit Conor's grave on Christmas morning, as they had been doing every year since his death. Instead, it was agreed that Christmas Eve was the more appropriate time for his parents and siblings to gather around his headstone and remember him, at the one time of the year when most families get together. 'Graveyard scenes are there all the time. They become a part of your life. You go, you pay homage and you lay down the flowers.' And at the Christmas dinner table, it is enough to mention his name. That's all we have to do; each of us knows instinctively what the other is thinking or feeling.' Batt shakes his head; his eyes glaze over. 'It's dreadful how much we miss him.'

The loss of what might have been is the thing that upsets Batt the most. 'He would have been twenty-two now, and I wonder what he would have been like. A few years would have made such a big difference. Now I'll never find out.'

Batt knew the boys who went to school with Conor. He sees them now as grown men. He watches them in the local pubs, enjoying a Friday night out, sharing a joke and a pint, and he tries to picture Conor standing there amongst them. 'Conor will never have a job. He had some girlfriends because he was into women like you wouldn't believe, but he'll never have a wife, a home of his own or a family. All that stuff that the rest of us accept as normal is gone forever, a chance blown. To me, it just seems so wasteful.'

Batt Coleman admits that at times Conor was a boisterous teenager. 'I was the guy who was hauling him back to make him behave. He was outgoing and familiar, with so much personality, full of chat. There was one occasion when Conor was stuck for words. It was after a match in Thurles, when his beloved Cork had just won the Munster hurling final. We were in Thurles and Seán Óg Ó hAlpín signed his jersey. It was the proudest moment of his short life.'

Conor had a huge interest in sport. He played football on the school team. He followed the Premiership but did not support the same team as Batt. 'He was a big Arsenal supporter and, since I'm a Liverpool supporter, we had many disagreements about that. Conor loved soccer. Cars, though, were his real passion. From a young age, he collected model cars.' Conor was counting the days until he could own a car of his own. But his last car journey was as a passenger, a fifteen-year-old boy, killed within three miles of his family home.

The last film the boys went to see at the cinema in Cork was *The Fast and the Furious*, an adrenalin-charged movie about fast cars. And the final conversation Conor had with Batt was about that film. Before leaving, Batt asked him what it was like, and Conor spoke his last words to his father: 'It's not your kind of movie, Dad.'

3

UNDER THE BONNETS OF THE BOY RACERS

'Every young lad has it in them, the need for speed.' Sean,* boy racer from Galway

His greatest fear is that he might lose his car, not his life. And, if he were to die, what better way to go than doing what he loves most: driving his fast Honda Civic. Twenty-year-old Sean, from Westside, Galway, is passionate about cars. For Sean and his friends, owning and driving a fast car is more than a hobby: it's a way of life. He is part of a group of more than fifty boy racers from Galway who meet regularly in a city-centre car park. This is where they socialise: not the pub, or the nightclub, but in the grounds of a supermarket when all the shoppers have gone.

It's a cold damp night in January 2009 when I meet the

* *Names have been changed in this chapter*

Galway 'crew', in an attempt to gain an insight into the psyche of the young men who cannot live without speed.

I sit in my car, watching and waiting. A broken trolley lies discarded near a green skip. A van driver munches on a burger; bits of sauce fall onto his lap, but he doesn't notice. Then I hear the sound of roaring exhausts. Boy racers are heard before they are seen. They arrive en masse, a convoy of modified motors, each driver hoping to prove that his car is the fastest.

Parking the car is a slick affair and, after making the figure of eight, Sean pulls up alongside a line of Honda Civics, the souped-up car of choice for these young drivers. None of the cars is new; some are almost as old as their eighteen-year-old owners. Once purchased, the vehicles are upgraded. Standard modifications include oversized exhausts, alloy wheels, short-shift gear sticks, black tinted windows and interior neon lighting. All the small front-wheel drive cars have been fitted with new engine parts, brakes and fuel systems. The suspension in each car has been lowered for better control and in order to enhance the aerodynamic performance, while body kits, including rear spoilers, wide tyres and flared wings, have also been fitted. If they were clothes, they would be ABBA outfits. The stereo systems are loud, like a nightclub. Techno tunes blare out of open windows into the frosty air.

'I spent four thousand euro on modifications to my car. I want my car to look sporty,' says Sean, as heat from the climate-controlled air vents blasts into his black coupé. Every cent he earns as a glazier goes towards the maintenance and upgrading of his prized possession. The car is black, slick, with tinted windows. Sean is happy to show it off. Dressed in a navy tracksuit, he walks around the car, pointing out the thick tyres, the shiny alloy wheels, fitted like miniature spaceships, and the spoiler, which reminds me of Dame Edna Everage's glasses. Sean is probably too young to remember the Australian drag queen.

He has been driving since the age of seventeen, and this is his third car in three years. He boasts about his crash-free record. 'The longer you go without crashing, the more confident you get. That's what happens with boy racers. I love fast cars and films about fast cars, like *The Fast and the Furious* and *Go*.' His eyes light up as he mentions the movies, and I can't help but wonder if he can tell the difference between the films and reality. Irresponsible, impulsive driving is one thing on the big screen, quite another on the main roads.

Sean would love to race his car on a proper rally track. In the absence of such a facility, the next best thing will do: the public road. This group of young drivers range in age from seventeen to twenty-four. That happens to be the age-bracket that is most at risk on the roads, accounting for a quarter of all road deaths in Ireland in 2008. Such statistics do not deter the Galway group from regularly revving up their engines and travelling together towards the dual carriageway on the outskirts of the city – the best place to race.

In Galway, invariably, the roads are damp, and the nights are windy – not exactly ideal driving conditions. One factor is crucial before a race: the road has to be empty. Most racing takes place after midnight along a short stretch of dual carriageway between Galway city and Oranmore village. Before each race, both sides of the carriageway are carefully checked for squad cars and other motorists. 'Because most of the cars are not rear-wheel drive, we need to race down straight roads. We usually go between eleven and one a.m. on any given night of the week,' explains Sean, who admits that lately, owing to a fatal crash involving a fellow boy racer, the group stopped racing every night.

'Our friend was killed. We all knew him and we don't want any more accidents.' Sean tells me about the fatal crash. 'It was at 8.45 in the morning, when the roads were full of traffic. Two boy racers pretended to have engine trouble, and stopped their cars on a roundabout along a dual carriageway, preventing any other traffic from overtaking. This gave them a clear stretch of road on one side. They took off, speeding. He wrapped himself around a pole and broke his neck. You don't race in traffic. Everyone knows that,' says Sean, with a sharp intake of breath. 'If there is a car on the road, lads don't race because they might scare someone. If there is an old person driving, we don't know how they are going to react to us. They could hit the brakes or swerve. So we drive up and down a couple of times to make sure the road is clear.'

But what about the vehicles which come along after the road has been checked? There are still huge risks involved. He cannot account for what could happen after a race starts, and he knows it: the parked tractor that might pull out from the hard shoulder, the BMW that joins the carriageway at speed. That sense of the unknown can enhance the thrill of racing on main roads.

Usually, a race attracts a crowd of boy racers, who act as both spectators and judges. There are two ways to begin a race: a rolling start, with both the cars in first gear, or a stop start, where both drivers take off simultaneously. With the windows wound down, a quick countdown signals the start of the race.

Nineteen-year-old John, a friend of Sean's, claims to have the fastest car. His 1.6 blue Honda Civic R Type certainly makes the most noise, and, in a recent race, it was the first past the post. 'You take off, neck and neck, and just plant the boot and go as fast as you can as far as the yellow bumper strips near the roundabout at the end of the dual carriageway – that's the finish line. You go up and down a few times and the best out of three is the better car, the faster car,' John explains. This is racing without the betting. Money does not change hands. Having the fastest car is the only prize worth winning. The coveted title amounts to nothing more than 'bragging' rights. John has another fundamental reason for racing: the adrenalin rush. 'It's a buzz really; just a thing that hits you. The point is to push the engines to 150 or 160 miles an hour, off the clock. You have to unleash the odd time against the other lads and go out on the "dualer". What we should have is a track. That would keep us off the road and everyone safe. You take risks here and there, overtaking stupidly, when you shouldn't,' says John. 'Being a boy racer is something to do; it's better than drinking or doing drugs.'

John believes he will crash at some stage in the future, and he has already had one lucky escape. 'I was racing one of my friends and he came flying up beside me and there was a truck coming towards us, so I had to brake and let him in, and when he was coming in, he nearly hit the truck and almost took the front off my car.' This close encounter gave the young supermarket worker 'a bit of a scare', but that's part of the thrill. A bigger scare is the gardaí. 'If they catch you, you can be banned off the road, and I need my car to get to work.'

Speaking also about the recent death of their friend, John recalls: 'It was dreadful. I was in school with him. He was racing when he died. He lost control.' John remembers the funeral, standing in the packed church, scanning the sea of young drivers. 'We all knew it could have been any of us.' Yet the death of one of their 'crew' has not caused these young men to give up their chosen pastime and membership in its subculture. It seems they are still oblivious to the extreme danger they face every time they put the boot down, as well as the threat they pose for other road users.

In January 2009, at an official car rally in Galway, hundreds of boy racers met up unofficially at 3 a.m. in a local industrial estate. A colourful sea of souped-up cars, some with fluorescent paint jobs, convened to parade their motors and watch the rear-wheel-drive racers perform doughnuts and drifting techniques. A doughnut is the act of rotating the rear of the car around the front wheels continuously by maintaining a high rev count while keeping the handbrake engaged. It can, if done right, create circular skid marks, causing lots of tyre smoke. It is a technique boy racers use solely to show off.

'Drifting' refers to a driving technique where the driver intentionally oversteers, causing loss of traction in the rear wheels through turns, while preserving vehicle control and a high speed. Boy racers could watch drifting displays like others watch movies, for hours on end. That night, under the glare of headlights, performers pirouetted for impressed onlookers. The displays were met with applause and cheering, both drowned out by the roar of the engines. 'The rally was excellent. Everyone was down for it. We got to meet boy racers from all over the country. We were all around the same age. The atmosphere was hard to beat,' John recalls. This illicit get-together could not have happened in broad daylight, and probably adds to the thrill of being a boy racer. I think they like breaking the rules. It strikes me that they see themselves as young rebels, irresponsible, impetuous and fearless.

Boy racers are not unique to Galway. Every county in Ireland is attempting to deal with this relatively new phenomenon. Car ownership in Ireland has doubled since 1990. Now, the first thing many teenagers look for once they reach the legal driving age is a car. The cost of insuring young male drivers is still sky high, but boy racers find innovative ways to keep down the price; many are named drivers on one or other of their parents' insurance. Some get insured on a cheaper car that allows them to drive any other car that is taxed and roadworthy. Otherwise, insurance could cost an average of close to €3,000 a year.

'When I got this car, I was quoted €2,900 to insure it. I'm on my mother's policy now, so it's only €900,' explains eighteen-year-old Brian from Westside in Galway. 'It's so hard for us because of the reputation we have. Basically, we have to try and find the cheapest option.'

An apprentice mechanic, Brian has always had an appreciation of and a passion for cars. He bought his 1998 Honda Civic coupé for €5,000. Blue neon lights flash at his feet, a decorative feature that especially impresses his girlfriend. Most of the extras were bought over the Internet or in motor part shops. 'You can buy anything from a body kit to an engine on the Internet.' Brian maintains that there is a skill involved in modifying cars. 'You have to have an idea of what you want, then go and find the parts, and if you're not able to fit them, you need to find someone who can. I know a number of "back garden" lads who fit parts here in Galway.'

Brian is one of the newest members of the Galway group, but was quickly made to feel welcome. He enjoys the camaraderie, the shared interests and the craic, and emphasises the social side of boy-racing, the side he feels goes unreported. 'When I first got this car, I knew only one or two people, but I drove down to the car park here and I made loads of friends. We come here all the time; we get a take-away burger and chips and we drive around. It's very much a social thing. We park the cars. Some nights, we just sit here for two to three hours, talking about our cars and what we've done to them. We do have a bad reputation. A few lads go out and race, but more of us just want to have nice cars. It's great if you have a car that has power. If you were going to overtake someone in a low-powered car, you'd have to get a run at them first. If you have a high-powered car, you can be right behind them, they could be driving really slowly and you just have to tap the accelerator and go past them.'

Brian then informs me that a driver is allowed to break the speed limit when overtaking. In fact, this is not true, but does not prevent him from believing it to be the case. Maybe it is just one of the excuses employed to justify his fast driving. 'It is just nice to know that you have power there if you want to use it. There is a bit of a thrill from it, when you do accelerate and you know your car can do it. I like speed, but I wouldn't go round driving fast for the sake of it. I try to stick to the speed limit and would only break it if there is a clear road ahead of me.'

Brian has been pulled over by the gardaí on a number of occasions. 'Some Guards are all right, and some of them you don't want to meet at all.' A garda caught him pulling handbrake turns in this car park. The technique involves turning the car rapidly around tight bends by locking up the rear wheels. It is used extensively in rally driving and should not be attempted on public roads. Brian was showing off. His girlfriend was in the passenger seat, while his friend was in the back seat. He apologised to the garda, not because he meant it, but because he knew it was the best thing to do. 'I told him I was stupid. I admitted it straight away. I told him I was messing with the handbrake. I could have lost control, but at five miles an hour, there was no chance of that happening.'

The illusion of control is a strongly held belief within the boy-racing community. It frightens me that these friendly young men have such confidence in their own driving abilities, that they remain ignorant of the inescapable fact: speed kills, over and over again. For those who still race, concentration is at the forefront of their minds. 'Racing requires your full attention,' says Sean, who has just returned from filling his high-powered car with petrol. 'All you see is the road in front of you. You're completely focused, in case anything does pull out.' He drives only around Galway city, but still spends an average of €90 a week on petrol.

The majority of the group claim never to drive when they have taken alcohol. However, as in other sections of society, drinking can be a problem within the boy-racing community. Sean explains that he had to take drastic action against one friend, who was intent on driving home drunk. 'My friend had been drinking all night. I had to block his car with my own car. I had no car for the night, but I had to make sure he wouldn't drive because he was in the middle of the town. He was a boy racer and he could have killed someone.'

Sean knows of others who smoke marijuana before driving home. 'They'd be able to drive their car home and park it up. They wouldn't be too stoned. Out of all the lads who come down here, there would be one or two who drive under the influence.' Sean, who says he doesn't drink or smoke, shakes his head in dismay at their attitude. He claims to firmly believe in staying sober. He assures me that boy racers get their kicks in other ways. It's a different type of drug, and they are all addicts. I want to make him see that speeding, or racing, even if it is just occasionally, is not an acceptable way to get his kicks. It's a lethal activity. I'm sure they have heard such advice before, and I'm also certain it has fallen on deaf ears. 'Every young lad has it in them. They like something fast; they like to keep going and going. It's addictive. When you're young, you want a fast car. You have friends who say they want to get a better car than you. It's a competition. You're going against each other all the time,' he says.

According to the Road Safety Authority, driver error is the main reason for road carnage; the majority of fatal crashes are caused by excessive speed. The daredevil tactics of young boy racers contribute to this carnage; yet each of these boy racers shares the belief that it will never happen to them, that they will not die or sustain terrible injuries in a car crash. When Sean considers the possibility that he might crash, his response is: 'I always say to the lads – if I die in a car, at least I was doing something I love doing: driving. It's a good way to go. I don't care. It doesn't bother me. When you're older, you might start to realise the dangers, the risks.'

While they are young, boy racers live life at a fast and furious pace, a fact that is often difficult for parents to accept. Sean admits that his mother worries about him all the time and has been especially concerned since the death of his friend in a car crash. Every time he leaves the house, he is warned to be careful on the roads. Sometimes, he says, his keys are confiscated or mysteriously go missing. 'She tells me, "Don't go racing. Don't do anything stupid." Sometimes she tells me, "Right, you're leaving your car here." But, it's my car. I don't think any of us really listen.'

Boy racers also come under fire for noise pollution. Those living in housing estates have to contend with regular complaints from the neighbours. This doesn't bother them too much, nor do they try to rectify the situation. 'When picking up speed on the open road, the sound of a roaring exhaust adds to the thrill of driving,' Sean explains, 'but whenever I'm going home, I have to crawl down my road at a snail's pace. The neighbours give out and have reported me to the Guards before.'

Dealing with a less-than-understanding public is an everyday occurrence for boy racers. They reject the idea that they may intimidate other road users. It seems that they refuse to see how a hundred loud cars congregating in a car park late at night or racing down a motorway behind unsuspecting drivers could be considered frightening. By the very nature of what they do, they are rash, young and selfish, and tend to always put themselves first. Passing their driving test is paramount. Having a full licence is especially important in case the gardaí pull them over.

On 29 October 2007, learner permits replaced provisional driving licences in Ireland. Car drivers with a learner permit must be accompanied at all times by someone who has had a full driving licence for at least two years. Learner permit holders must also display L-plates on their car at all times, and no boy racer wants that particular sticker on show. 'If you have a boy racer car, then the Guards are more likely to stop you, so you're better off having a full licence, or face a lot of hassle,' says Sean. 'Everybody is against boy racers. No one will ever stick up for us. No one in a car like mine will ever tell you that he likes the Guards. A Guard will stop every Honda Civic. I could be driving within the speed limit and a normal car could overtake me and the Guards will still pull me in because of how my car looks.'

Sean ensures his car is always in perfect condition, because, above all else, he fears being put off the road. 'I don't want any Guard to find fault with my car or catch me speeding. I have no fear, except about losing my licence. I want to drive, so I watch the speed limit.' Watching it and adhering to it are two different things.

The temptation to put the boot down is still strong, especially when Sean comes across another modified car on a main road. He explains that the driver could be a stranger, but his own competitive streak sometimes takes over. 'You might see another boy racer car beside you and think "my car could beat that", and so you might try to keep up with it. A race can start like that. It's not really planned. If you went fast enough, he might come after you. You just race until one of you gives up.'

Sean also gets competitive with other unsuspecting motorists, who happen to overtake him. 'I was driving on the dual carriageway and an Audi overtook me. If you know you can beat a car, you don't like it passing you out, so you go after it.' Racing strangers can be arranged via Internet chatrooms and social networking sites. Some drivers choose to leave 'For Sale' signs on their cars with mobile phone numbers. This can be interpreted as an 'invitation' to race, but it is an offer Sean says he has never taken up.

Being a boy racer is all about image. These youngsters believe that driving souped-up cars can attract women. 'It's a definite babe magnet and does impress the girls,' Sean says, 'As for girl racers in Galway, there are one or two who have cars, but they don't drive as well as we do.'

At this stage, I decide to take a spin with Sean, who drives out to the dual carriageway. He picks up speed. I'm sitting in the back and I have to shout over the roar of the exhaust. He pulls in to the hard shoulder to show me just how fast his car can clock up speed. We drive off and within ten seconds, the speedometer has hit sixty miles an hour. I brace myself as he puts the pedal down and we overtake every other car on the road. He stays in the fast lane. Make no mistake about it: this is his territory. The engine noise gets louder, like a plane before take-off. It is singing to him, and I think that this must be the sweetest sound in the world to him and boy racers everywhere. But my heart is in my mouth. This is not thrilling; this is insane.

Boy racers are often described in the media as drivers who regard their cars as toys and driving as a game. Figures from RAC Ireland reflect this portrayal: 22 per cent of drivers under the age of twenty-five already have penalty points. Between 2000 and 2008, figures also showed that twenty-seven underage drivers were killed on the country's roads.

The Chairman of the Road Safety Authority, Gay Byrne, fears that the road safety message is lost on this section of society. 'All over the world, not just in Ireland, the pattern is precisely the same – the 17- to 25-year-old male is the most dangerous person on the road. And the experience in other countries is that you can advertise till you're blue in the face, you can also advise them, but there is a particular difficulty in the psychological and psychiatric make-up of young men of that age-group which leaves them in particular danger and exposed to fatal crashes.'

Gay Byrne thinks that trying to target young men with hard-hitting road safety advertisements is possibly a waste of money. 'When this particular group set out to drive a car, they have four delusions. First, "I am immortal"; second, "I am invulnerable"; third, "bad things happen to other people, they don't happen to me"; and finally, when it comes to driving a car, "I am every bit as good as Lewis Hamilton, if not better".'

Crucially, he believes that young men in that age-group have no fear. 'The part of the frontal lobe of the brain, which works on people to warn them of danger, is slower developing in young men than in young women.' Byrne admits that, although these young men appreciate the message of the Road Safety Authority, when they get behind the wheel of a car, they do not associate the message with themselves; rather, with everyone else.

Defending the position of the boy racers, Sean dismisses what Gay Byrne has to say. When asked what he thinks of the former veteran broadcaster, Sean says, 'I don't think of him.' His friend John agrees, 'I don't really listen to what Gay Byrne has to say.'

This group of young men are determined to stay on the road. For now, they are married to their cars; there is no room for anything else. They are faithful and loving car-owners, taking immense pride in their modified motors and how fast they can drive them. Losing a close friend to a racing collision has caused them pain. They claim to have learned from this tragic crash, but as they prepare to drive home on this January night, Sean says that they might try to keep up with each other. 'You can hardly class that as racing,' he states, before driving off in a cloud of exhaust fumes.

4

'I COULD HAVE BEEN A KILLER . . .'

'I had written my political obituary. I knew that when I rang Bertie Ahern's office the morning after my arrest.' Dr Jim McDaid

D r Jim McDaid considers himself a lucky man. On the night of 26 April 2005, the former government minister was behind the wheel of his car, driving along the wrong side of the Naas dual carriageway. The blinding lights of cars sped past him. At first, Dr McDaid was oblivious to the dangers. His mind was fuzzy, his thoughts unfocused; he kept blinking. A haze of alcohol had distorted his reality. He was driving while more than three times over the legal alcohol limit.

People started to honk their horns. A sea of vehicles rushed towards his car. He could feel his heart race, pounding against his ribcage. Checking the rear-view mirror, he realised the slip road he had just come off was too far back and so he ruled out reversing. Keeping well into the hard shoulder, Dr McDaid concentrated. Beads of sweat had started to form on his forehead. Leaning forward, he squinted. If he drove at a slow pace, he might just make it out of this nightmare. The next turn off from the dual carriageway couldn't be that far. He would keep going, driving towards Naas. The vibrations of the passing traffic shook his car. His hands gripped the steering wheel. This time, he had gone too far. How, he wondered, would he get away with this stunt? He didn't.

Drink-driving is pervasive in Ireland. Every day people are banned from driving as a result of being drunk at the wheel. In courtrooms across the country, businessmen hang their heads in shame, teenage van drivers curse judges in hushed tones, ordinary people get their licences revoked. One of the most high-profile drink-driving cases ever to come before the courts was that of Dr Jim McDaid.

'Named and shamed' is a clichéd phrase, but it still has the power to make news editors salivate. The premise is simple: when the public know your name and you fall from grace in a shameful manner, the report of it is going to sell newspapers. The news of Dr McDaid getting caught drink-driving was the perfect media storm. 'My face was on the front page of every newspaper for weeks; I turned on the television and I would see myself,' he says. His eyes widen when he speaks, as if he is still unable to grasp why his story was such big news. The media interest eventually eased, but Dr McDaid claims that he still shudders at the thought of what might have been.

A doctor since 1974, the only nightmares he ever used to experience concerned his medical finals. Now, his sleepless nights centre on the carnage he could have caused by drunken driving. The Donegal North-East Dáil deputy has been in politics since 1989. Despite his many professional and political achievements, Dr McDaid believes he will always be known as the 'drunken politician'. 'No matter what I'm quoted on, no matter what the subject matter, I'm always referred to as the former government minister who drove the wrong way down the dual carriageway. But that's a good thing. Those journalists are reminding me of what I did and I need to be reminded. They are serving a purpose. It's just like going to an AA meeting; I'm being reminded of my deficiencies.'

Ballyliffin village, on the coast of Donegal, forms part of the Inishowen Peninsula. Five hotels, left over from the Celtic Tiger, line the hilly street. I meet Dr McDaid in the newly built Ballyliffin Lodge. The open-plan lounge is bright and modern, with light wooden floors. It is also empty. Large bay windows offer sea views. Frothy waves hit the sandy shoreline. It is February 2009 and the stretch in the evenings is at last noticeable. The sky is a diluted blue. Gulls fly low in the late evening light, as the sun begins to slip behind the snow-capped mountains. Dusk strokes the sky, bribing daylight into darkness.

Sitting in a leather-studded armchair, Dr McDaid shifts in his seat, crossing and uncrossing his legs, as he recalls the night he wrote his political epitaph. The slim, white-haired public representative is dressed in a striped navy jumper and navy chinos. He tells me that his holiday home is just minutes away and that he loves Ballyliffin. I get the impression he would much rather talk about Donegal.

He sighs when asked to recount the day of his arrest,

then scratches the back of his head. 'I think it's well documented what happened on that day,' he begins. 'I left Donegal at six a.m. for a dental appointment in Dublin. I was under general anaesthetic for the procedure but chose not to lie down to rest afterwards. I went back to Leinster House. I didn't have much to do. I got a call from friends of mine, who offered me the chance to get a helicopter ride to the Punchestown Races in Kildare. I drove to Citywest near the Naas dual carriageway, where I parked up my car and got the chopper to the course.'

While at the races, Dr McDaid, a well-known racing enthusiast, placed a few bets, won and lost some money, and availed of the hospitality in the corporate tent. He enjoyed an afternoon of free wine and also drank a number of pints of Guinness. 'I had been fasting because of the general anaesthetic. I had drunk water up until four o'clock, but then I started on the wine and Guinness. I left in the helicopter, and I was drunk.'

On his return to Citywest, he decided to take a taxi back to the Burlington Hotel in Dublin where he was staying. Five minutes into the journey, he realised he'd left his overnight bag and change of clothes in his car. He asked the taxi driver to turn back. The next decision he made was the worst of his life. 'I was taking the things out of my car and I thought, to hell with it, I'm okay. I gave the driver twenty euro and I said, "I'll drive". The rest is history.'

At 10.30 that night, Dr McDaid was arrested close to Naas after driving erratically for up to ten miles along the wrong side of the dual carriageway. The potentially fatal episode ended only after the driver of an articulated lorry used his truck to block two lanes, forcing Dr McDaid to stop. What possessed him to drive in the condition he was in? He was clearly drunk, his judgement impaired. The signposts on the roundabouts along the dual carriageway confused him, but Dr McDaid is careful to stress that this was no excuse for getting it wrong:

'That morning, I swear to you that I drove the wrong way onto the dual carriageway from the same roundabout close to Citywest. That night, with the drink taken, there was no hope of me getting it right. I can remember seeing "Northbound" and I wanted to go northbound, but the next thing I knew there were cars coming towards me.'

As the oncoming traffic sped past him, Dr McDaid says that he knew in his heart and soul that he was going to be caught. 'If I saw cattle on the road, or an obstruction of any kind, I tend to call the local Garda station and I knew there was bound to be somebody who would definitely call the Guards to report me.' At this stage, he was not thinking about the carnage he could have caused. His main priority was to get off the road in one piece. The full political and professional consequences of his irresponsible actions had not yet dawned on him. He was still drunk and suddenly worried that he was more than likely going to be arrested. That happened at the next exit at Ladytown, Naas, when his path was blocked.

'When I got off the wrong side of the carriageway, I let out a sigh of relief. I was like, hey, I'm off it. Then the truck driver blocked me – fair play to him. A Guard pulled up beside me and the sergeant said, "I want to take control of this car." I was taken to Naas Garda Station where I gave blood.'

Dr McDaid's blood alcohol level showed 267 mg of alcohol per 100 ml of blood, more than three times over the legal limit of 80 mg of alcohol per 100 ml of blood. He was put into a small holding cell. While behind bars, he admits that at first the gravity of what had just happened failed to hit him. Still numbed by the amount of alcohol he had taken, he chose to lie down on the bed and rest. It was uncomfortable; the place had a sterile smell. His mouth, stained black from red wine, was dry. He asked for a glass of water. He was then allowed to make one phone call. Dr McDaid called his brother, Hughie, in Donegal, who assured him he would drive down to collect him later that night.

'I just lay down and waited for him to come. I didn't sleep. You don't sleep. I knew it would take my brother five hours. As the night wore on, I started to wonder what I was going to tell my partner and family. I knew it was going to be in the media.'

What Dr McDaid did not know at that stage was just how much it was going to dominate the national press. He was front-page news for almost two weeks. The story did not end until after his court appearance in October 2005. Indeed, it is one of those shameful episodes that may never disappear from the public consciousness. In 2008, Today FM broadcast an item on its satirical show *Gift Grub*, in which the Taoiseach Brian Cowen asks who is going to drive the cabinet home. Dr Jim McDaid answers that he will be the chauffeur, but he just has to get drunk first. This joke is one of many known to Dr McDaid, who is able to laugh at them now. In the aftermath of his arrest, however, he thought he might never laugh again.

'It was desperate. I sat in the house for days. I felt rotten. I didn't shave. When I turned on the television, I was headline news. I felt things were being grossly exaggerated in some places. Even though there were other things happening in the news, I was the front page for nine consecutive days. I was called a "disgrace" and an "idiot".' He moped around the house, unable to motivate himself to go outside, lying instead on the sofa in his dressing gown. He knew his political life had effectively come to an end.

'I had written my political obituary,' Dr McDaid says. 'I knew that. I rang Bertie Ahern's office at 10 a.m. the morning after my arrest. I told them what had happened and I apologised. They had to release a statement on my behalf.' Details of the drink-driving incident emerged just as Bertie Ahern called on motorists to drive responsibly during the forthcoming bank holiday weekend. He was speaking in the Dáil just as Dr McDaid was working on his statement.

It was also revealed that Dr McDaid, who had been Junior Minister with responsibility for road traffic from 2002 to 2004, had been in charge of a drink-driving clampdown in 2002, when he had declared that drunken driving cost innocent lives. 'Some people are continuing to ignore our drink-driving laws,' he said then. These statements came back to haunt him. Dr McDaid did not turn to any political colleagues at the time. 'I didn't go to the Dáil for nearly a month. I waited to let things die down.'

It was not just his political life that was ruined: his reputation as a doctor was also in tatters. 'I just wanted to bury myself. Each news story about me that I watched made me feel even more down. I was so low. It was embarrassing, particularly for a person in the medical profession. It was a terrible time for my family, my political party and my profession,' he recalls. Steeped in feelings of shame and humiliation, Dr McDaid decided one day to 'face the music'. He realised he had to accept and move on from his gross error of judgement.

'I said to myself: I'm getting up today and I'm shaving and I'm going to walk from one side of the town to the other and face people again.' Cautiously, he ventured out that lunchtime to walk through the town of Letterkenny, where his practice is based. At first, he was afraid to look people in the eye. The pavements were packed with shoppers and office workers. Middle-aged women with bags of groceries brushed past him. Suited office workers peered at menus in café windows. Mothers scolded petulant toddlers. School-uniformed teenagers laughed loudly at their own jokes. Traffic had built up in the centre of town and some motorists honked their horns in frustration.

Dr McDaid slowly lifted his head and nodded meekly at the passers-by. He was not shouted down at every turn. In fact, many of his constituents approached him with words of encouragement, admitting that they, too, had made similar mistakes but, unlike him, they had never been caught. 'Life continued on around me, with people paying little or no heed to me on my walk of shame. You think everybody is continuing to talk about you, but they seemed preoccupied with themselves. A few people asked how I was doing. Leaving the house and facing the public, after all those days stuck inside, wallowing and worried, was the best thing I could have done at the time.'

Dr McDaid stopped drinking after his arrest. He admits that his relationship with alcohol has always caused him difficulties. He had often disgraced himself in public, at race meetings and even at political functions. His family has been let down more times than he cares to remember, and all because of that one glass too many. His first marriage ended, largely because of problems associated with his alcoholism. If he opened a bottle of whiskey, he would want to finish it. 'I could never see the point in leaving a bottle half-full. I'm a binge drinker.'

Dr McDaid was off the drink when Bertie Ahern appointed him Minister for Sport and Tourism in 1997 and he stayed off it for several years, his most successful period in politics. When he was dropped from the front bench in 2002, he was distraught. The junior ministry in transport was a consolation prize. Dr McDaid was soon drinking off and on again. He has attended Alcoholics Anonymous intermittently for years. After his arrest, he once again took part in regular meetings. The night of 26 April 2005 caused him to question his actions.

Dr McDaid shudders slightly, gazing into the middle distance, 'I could have been a killer. I don't know how I would have lived having killed somebody. I think it would have finished me. I was lucky. I think I have my mother's prayers to thank. She's a very holy woman, and prays for her children daily, that they may be safe and kept out of trouble. Her prayers were obviously answered. I'm so thankful. I'm relieved.'

The interview is interrupted, a welcome interlude. Neal, his three-year-old son, runs into the hotel bar. He sits on his father's lap, a blond smiling boy, with ruddy cheeks and long lashes. Bored within minutes, he takes a chocolate biscuit from a saucer on the table before running out to play again. Dr McDaid has four children with his first wife, Marguerite. Nicola, Garreth, Jason and Luke range in age from thirty-nine to twenty. He married again in October 2007 and he and Siobhan O'Donnell have one child, Neal.

As a doctor, Dr McDaid has had first-hand experience of road crashes. Earlier in his career, he worked as a surgeon in emergency medicine at Letterkenny General Hospital, where he regularly dealt with victims of road traffic collisions. In more recent years, he was often called to the scenes of crashes along the roads of Donegal. 'I've seen legs, arms, body parts, and bones all over the place. I've witnessed total mutilation. I've even had a man with a ruptured spleen die in front of me on the roadside.' He knows what irresponsible driving can do. He knows, too, that surviving a car crash can sometimes be a life sentence in itself:

'I still get flashbacks of that night. When I saw those cars flying at me, even though I was close to the verge, it would not have taken much for them to hit me. I can still see what could have happened and on a dual carriageway it could have been a multiple collision. There is no question that I have nightmares. I did have initially, and still do. It makes it all the more harrowing for me because I have seen people who have survived car smashes. I know the mutilation I could have caused. I certainly don't know how I could have possibly lived knowing that somebody down in Kildare was in a wheelchair as a result of me driving drunk that day or how I could have gone back to work and got on with my life. Because of my driving, someone could have been left with no quality of life.'

Many road crash victims spend time in the National Rehabilitation Centre in Dun Laoghaire, County Dublin, where they learn to adjust to life with a serious spinal or brain injury. Dr McDaid has spent time in that hospital, and has met patients who will never walk again. The fact that he could have paralysed someone crosses his mind most days. 'My sister had a brain haemorrhage,' he explains. 'She was in Dun Laoghaire, where I used to visit her. I got to know people in the hospital. I've seen the patients who were there because of drunk drivers.'

He says his heart goes out to these injured victims. Controversially, he also believes that, in some cases, it would be better for survivors of road crashes to have died. 'I could have killed someone that night, but I think if I had have killed somebody it would have been better for them because I think that the people who actually survive are sometimes far worse off than the people who die. We rarely talk about the numbers of people who are maimed and in wheelchairs. We never hear about those figures. There is never any contact between the perpetrator and the victims, apart from the actual court cases. They live separate lives, and they never get to see how the injured people are left to cope.'

Naas Courthouse stands on the main street of Kildare's county town. It is a yellow and cream building, with Roman pillars and steps leading to an imposing double door, the only way in and out of the courthouse. On the morning of 12 October 2005, a large crowd had gathered. Television crews, journalists and photographers lined the wide steps, as excited locals looked on, taking in the media frenzy. It was a bright, dry day. Inside the courthouse, every seat was taken, occupied mainly by reporters, who sat in rows, pens and notebooks at the ready.

Dr Jim McDaid was fully aware that his court appearance would be flagged in every newsroom across the country. There was no escaping the public interest in his case. 'This was not a particularly big courthouse,' he says. 'I was told that, normally, the back four or five rows would be empty at any given sitting, but that morning the place was packed with media. My case came up. I think the Judge couldn't understand the amount of attention that surrounded it. He asked was I present in court. I said I was and pleaded guilty to two drink-driving related charges: dangerous driving and drunken driving.'

Through his solicitor, Brian Pierce, Dr McDaid told the court, 'There is no reason or excuse for my doing what I did. To get behind the wheel of a motor vehicle in my condition was a disgrace. It is something that I will never forget. Regretfully, I shall never be allowed to forget it. I'll accept whatever punishment is deemed appropriate.'

Judge Murrough Connellan said Dr McDaid was 'extremely lucky' that nobody was injured. He fined him €250 for driving under the influence of alcohol and €500 for dangerous driving at Ladytown, Naas, County Kildare. Two other charges of dangerous driving were struck out. Dr Jim McDaid was also disqualified from driving for two years.

As he left the courthouse, journalists swooped on the disgraced Dáil deputy. 'There was a barrage of microphones and cameras before me as I walked from the court. The tabloids had called me a number of derogatory names – things like idiot – and I told them they were right. I was all those things they had branded me on that day. What more could I say?' He stood on the steps of the courthouse and announced that he was full of regret and remorse over his actions, particularly given his role as a legislator.

Once satisfied with the sound bite, the swarm of reporters dispersed. Dr McDaid left the town of Naas that morning, glad to close this chapter of his life. 'I was thankful; I was relieved. I didn't give a damn about the disqualification. I got what I deserved. I did my sentence and I paid my debt to society. There was only me to blame. I can make all the excuses in the world. The fact of the matter was I should not have got into that car.'

The drink-driving episode is his biggest regret, but he has learned from his mistake. 'When you regret something, it just means that you're sorry. When you have remorse for something, you are determined that it will never happen again. I'm certainly remorseful from that point of view. You don't understand how grateful I am that I'm able to sit here today and still laugh. My character has been torn apart, but I didn't kill or maim anyone.'

Drink still plays a role in his life. During his time as Minister for Tourism, the deputy stopped drinking for seven years. He says that he could list off a multitude of reasons why he started drinking again, ranging from losing his ministerial post to the breakdown of his marriage, but that he knows, in the end, they are excuses. Despite the difficulties drinking can present for Dr McDaid, he still enjoys a tipple, especially at major sporting events, like the races at Cheltenham or the Aintree Grand National.

'I'm able to drink,' he says. 'I still enjoy it. I regret it afterwards, because it doesn't suit me. It never has. If I get drunk, I make a fool of myself. When I get drunk now, I know I'm not in control of my faculties. If I'm premeditating going on a binge, I always make sure my car is not within reach. If I go to the Dáil to have a drink, I leave my car at the hotel. I don't take any chances.'

Dr McDaid admits that he no longer drinks very often, 'I might drink once or twice a month and then I would have three or four months without any. It's a well-known fact that I have a drink problem.'

The night Dr McDaid was caught driving the wrong way on the Naas dual carriageway was not the first time he had been driving while under the influence. He says that, throughout his life, he has taken chances and there have been other times when he has been behind the wheel of a car in 'far from ideal circumstances'. He recalls driving to parties as a student, with his car full of friends and beers, a time when perhaps it was easier to get away with drink-driving.

But how much have attitudes really changed? After his arrest, Dr McDaid found that many people living in rural constituencies sympathised with him. 'They'd say to me, "There go I but for the grace of God". You'll always get your critics, but some people came up to me and said "We did it, we were not caught".' He fears that too many people are still getting away with drinking and driving in Ireland.

'I think the judiciary are too lenient with drink-driving. Because of technical points, there are not enough convictions. The dangers of drinking and driving need to be drummed into young people. Transition-year students should be brought to the National Rehabilitation Centre in Dun Laoghaire to see at first hand the tragic consequences of car crashes. It would be more relevant than bringing them to some ski slope.'

Dr McDaid says he will never drink and drive again. The general practitioner, who has one of the largest practices in County Donegal, has kept every newspaper clipping concerning his arrest and subsequent court case in 2005; scrapbooks full of reminders of the man he used to be.

When Brian Cowen was tipped to become the next Taoiseach in May 2008, Dr Jim McDaid approached him with no expectations. 'I said, "I'm coming to you saying that I'm not looking for anything, because I have written my political obituary with my drink-driving episode. I wouldn't first of all expect you to appoint me to anything nor would I expect to be appointed to anything." I cleared the air, just before he became Taoiseach. His response was one of quiet acceptance.'

Dr McDaid believes he has had a good twenty years in Irish politics. He announced his retirement from political life in 2006, but reversed his decision following the announcement that Independent TD Niall Blaney was to join Fianna Fáil. In the last general election, Dr McDaid ran and was elected on a Fianna Fáil ticket. His drink-driving shame was no bar to re-election, just to ministerial appointment. He was still the favourite candidate and his potentially fatal mistake did not deter enough of the electorate from voting for him. It appears that for parts of the population, at least, the problem of drink-driving could be treated in a more serious manner.

In November 2008, he abstained from voting with the government on a cervical cancer vaccination programme and thereby lost the parliamentary whip. 'I maintain that by not providing this service, the government has in effect passed a death sentence on a certain percentage of these twelve-year-old girls whose parents could not afford the €650 cost of getting the vaccine privately.'* Now waiting to get back into the party fold, Dr McDaid's days on the front bench are finished. Through the bad times, his constituents have supported him: 'When the next general election came along after my drink-driving conviction, I was re-elected. There is a sense of loyalty, and I think you'll find that a lot of people will say that they did the same thing – they were in my position, drunk behind the wheel of a car, but they were not caught.'

* In January 2010, the government reversed its decision and announced that a cervical cancer vaccination programme would be rolled out for up to 30,000 first-year schoolgirls by the summer.

5

A SURVIVOR'S STORY

'People don't know how to react to you if you have a brain injury; they're thinking, oh God, he's a mutant.' Micilín Feeney

The coastal road to Connemara is busy with tourist traffic; heaving coaches with no care for dividing lines, and brand new Fiat Puntos. The only people on the road with new cars are those not used to driving on the left-hand side of it: tanned sightseers ambling by in their hire motors, at forty miles an hour, regularly mistaking the wipers for indicators. At least the sun is shining, I think, as I pull into the forecourt at Spidéal to buy some new batteries for my Dictaphone.

Barefoot children with matted curls and filthy faces are playing a game of chasing in the shop. Their mother doesn't seem to care that her urchin-like offspring have a distinct look of Oliver Twist about them. I buy what I need and leave.

Across the street, a swimmer glides through the sea, slicing the surface with elongated strokes. Teenagers from the local Irish college tiptoe towards the salty lather at the water's edge. The *Bean an Tí* will call them soon for a supper of beans, chips and overcooked pork chops. My life-long aversion to tomato sauce began at Irish college. I watch the reeds bend slightly to let the light breeze pass, and inhale the treacle-thick smell of seaweed. It invigorates me, momentarily.

Spidéal soon gives way to a barren road. I take a sharp turn towards unspoilt beauty, a straight stretch of tarmac without bungalows or holiday cottages. It could lead to the end of the world. Hidden lakes lie between the rocks. Sheep wander close to or on the road. I swerve to avoid a mindless ram. The Twelve Pins dominate the intense blue skyline ahead; streaks of violet decorate the impressive mountain range like laser lighting.

I take the turn for Lettermullan, a remote area of Connemara cut off from the rest of the coastline by a series of narrow bridges. The region is also known as 'the Islands'. I have come here to meet someone who should not be alive. Micilín Feeney was given the last rites. He was in a coma for four months. His family were told that he had a higher chance of dying than of living. They got Micilín back, but it was not the brother or son they had always known. In October 2004, Micilín crashed his car. The 23-year-old survived, but suffered a brain injury.

I arranged to meet Micilín at the small village church, on a hill overlooking the ocean. This was where he had intended to get married. That was before his crash, when he had a fiancée. A car approaches from the far side of the bridge; Micilín sits in the passenger seat. He moves to get out of the car, but I tell him to stay put.

'I'll follow you,' I shout out of my window. He gives me the thumbs-up sign. I follow the car off the main thorough-fare and on to a narrow road towards the Feeney family home. I notice the grass tracks along the middle. The sea is always close, the toss and turn of the green tide breaking on the shoreline. June sunlight dances on the water; the ocean is a giant mirror-ball. A patchwork of stone walls reaches out in every direction, claiming rocky ground.

Micilín greets me when we reach the grey stone bungalow, the house where he grew up. His palms were once the rough hands of a working man. Now they are soft, their grip poor. I do not get to meet the driver of the car, his brother, P. J. He doesn't like to talk about what happened to Micilín, least of all to a journalist.

'You can sit yourself down there. Very pleased to meet you, Jenny.' Micilín indicates a chair by the table. The room is basic, untouched by the trappings of the Celtic Tiger boom. Damp clothes – jeans, jumpers and socks – lie in a stack on top of a cream range. I leave my bag on the linoleum floor. A well-worn armchair with a distinct depression in the middle sits beside the range. This, Micilín later tells me, is his seat, where he watches television, which is what he does all day, every day.

On the windowsill, I look at photographs of the family in younger days, gap-toothed smiles from behind a brown Ford Cortina, Micilín and his three younger siblings: brother P. J. and twins, John and Noreen. Next to a statue of St Patrick stands another framed picture, this time of a handsome, blond man at his school debs, surrounded by laughing friends, brandishing pints of Guinness. I can almost feel the fun emanate from the photograph, taste the joy in their eyes of crushed diamonds. I stare at the photograph, trace the face with my forefinger and wonder if that is the same person as the man standing next to me.

'That was me at my debs,' says Micilín. 'That was a great night.' Micilín was a young man who enjoyed many great nights. 'I worked hard and played hard,' he tells me, adopting a slightly acerbic tone. 'That was my problem. I played too hard and was stupid. I was foolish. I just didn't think this could happen to me.' He excuses himself to get some notes: worn typed pages of bullet points outlining what has happened to him, in chronological order, since the night of his crash. Not that he needs them. He cannot forget how his life changed irrevocably in the space of a few seconds on Halloween night 2004.

Micilín, who was a keen GAA footballer, had been to a match earlier that day between local rivals, Carraroe and his beloved Lettermullan. He played for Lettermullan, but on this occasion was not part of the squad. The drinking began mid-afternoon, when a group of supporters gathered at the local pub. Micilín continued to drink pints of cider for the rest of the night. He was in high spirits, playing cards with his friends, looking forward to catching up with his fiancée later that evening at their shared home nearby. He never made it back. Instead, after what he terms a 'skinful' of pints, he left the pub and before long crashed his car. 'I have work tomorrow, lads. I'm off.' These were the last words the 23-year-old spoke before his crash.

I stay for an hour, refusing tea or coffee. I probe for more information, greedy for it. Micilín sticks to his script

74

because he cannot deviate from it. As he freely admits, on an emotional level, things will never be the same again for him. Physically, he walks with a tremor, dragging his feet. His throat has a hole, which will not heal, from the feeding tube he used for five months. His speech has the slurred hallmark of a drunk. Emotionally, he is a different person. This is the greatest tragedy.

'All I want for the future is a wife, a place of my own and kids, definitely kids, nothing too complicated.' I cannot help but feel that this dream will be difficult for him to realise. He is twenty-eight now, still handsome, but not the man he once was. In some respects, he says he is more sociable, friendlier, and open to new things. But few new things come his way, apart from the information talks he gives to schools on the dangers of drink-driving.

Micilín had the world at his feet, a beautiful fiancée, a place of his own, a steady job as a builder and a Gaelic football record to be proud of with his local club, Letter-mullan. The year he crashed, he had been voted Player of the Year. 'The irony of it,' he says. 'I drank to excess. I think I fell asleep at the wheel. I woke up five months later in a Galway hospital.'

I cannot imagine what it must feel like to lose what he has lost. 'I used to drive home drunk a lot, ever since I got my car, six months before the crash.' He speaks in a matter of fact way, as if driving home drunk was the most normal thing in the world. To him it once was.

Micilín shows me a blown-up picture of the car he was driving, a blue Mazda 323. It is unrecognisable. Sheets of twisted metal make up the wreckage. 'Can you believe I came out of that alive?' he asks.

Micilín could have died that night. He can never be sure, but he believes he fell asleep at the wheel. 'There was nothing else on the road, just me being drunk. I don't remember how many pints I'd had but my weekends typically would have involved a lot of drinking. I was about three or four times over the legal limit. I started drinking at about four in the afternoon and I left the pub at around 11.40 p.m. I was about four miles from my home. I crashed on the main road, midway between the pub and my house. I was living with my girlfriend at the time in Bealadangan, close to Lettermullan and about four miles from the pub where I'd been socialising.'

Fortunately, there were no passengers in the car with Micilín. He often dropped friends home, but not on this occasion. His Mazda 323 left the road at speed and crashed into a wall before tumbling into a derelict building on the other side of it. He had bought the 1992 model six months before the crash. It was his first car and would be his last. The car's headlights continued to work following the smash.

Minutes after the crash, the local undertaker was driving towards the scene when he noticed beams of lights in the distance. He drove closer and saw that the light was coming from the derelict building. He knew immediately something was wrong. Moments later he discovered Micilín fighting for breath in the mangled wreckage.

Micilín has been told everything about the next four months of his life second-hand. He has no clear memories of anything between 31 October 2004 and 14 February 2005. For much of this time he was in a deep coma, except for a short period at Christmas. His first distinct memory is Valentine's Day 2005, his birthday. Waking up from the coma was a surreal experience. He remembers an occupational therapist dressed in a white uniform hovering close to his bed. She was holding something out to him, an item with a flickering flame. It was an iced bun with a candle on it for his twenty-fourth birthday. He reached out to take the cake and regained consciousness. For Micilín, it was like seeing everything for the first time. He was told that he was safe, that he was being looked after in Galway University Hospital. Over the next few weeks and months, the full extent of what had happened to him became clear. He had to learn how to live with an acquired brain injury. His family would also have to learn to let go of the Micilín they had known all their lives and learn to accept his injuries and their consequences.

The doctors in Galway explained to Micilín that, immediately after the crash, he was rushed to hospital in Galway, before being transferred to Beaumont Hospital in Dublin.

'In Dublin, my mother was told that there was more chance that I would die than live, but I came to. She was also told that I would never walk again, but I can walk. She was told that I would find it very difficult to speak again, but I'm talking to you now,' says Micilín. He is triumphant, and I'm happy to see him rejoice in his achievements, none of which was easy.

At first Micilín's ability to walk, talk, or even to feed himself was extremely limited. His short- and long-term memory was poor. It will never be as sharp as it was. He had no idea that his father was dead, and had to learn this devastating news all over again from his then fiancée.

'Three weeks before my crash, I lost my Dad to lung

cancer. It sent me off the rails. I was very close to him. I had just buried my Dad and I nearly buried myself,' he says. Did it make sense that he was behaving so recklessly on the night of the crash? Could the raw grief have played a part in his irresponsible choices that evening? Micilín thinks it could have influenced his behaviour, but admits that drink-driving amongst young people in Connemara was not unusual at the time. There was more bad news to come. Micilín discovered that his best friend and teammate on the Lettermullan football team had also died in a car crash while Micilín was in the coma. This had a huge impact on him, and for years he has been coping with strong feelings of guilt for having survived a car crash, when his best friend did not. 'I remember hearing this news. I could not speak properly at the time and so could not express myself. I was totally shocked. I could talk in my head, in both Irish and English, but could not get the words out. I would get so frustrated with myself.'

Further frustration was to follow, when Micilín finally realised that he was never going to be the same as he had been. He was transferred to the National Rehabilitation Hospital in Dun Laoghaire in County Dublin in April 2005 to be treated for his brain injury. The three-month stint there helped him to adapt to a new way of life. It would take much longer to finally let go of the old one.

During his second month in Rehab, Micilín was determinedly walking down the corridor unaided. Just putting one foot in front of the other took such a tremendous effort. Even when he managed it, he looked unsteady. Mind over matter, he told himself as he struggled to make it to the end of the hall. He almost fell, reaching out to the bar at the wall to prevent himself from toppling over. He stood still, gripping the handrail, fighting a feeling he couldn't quite place, and at that moment he realised that no amount of practice was going to give him back what he had lost. In his head he said, 'Nah, not the same old Micilín.'

'That's when it dawned on me that life as I knew it was over. And that *hurt*. I felt terrible. At the time, I didn't even cry. Emotions just passed me by. They get to me now a bit more than they did then. Up until that moment, the entire time I was in there, I was thinking I will soon get out of here and be fine, go back to work as a bricklayer and once again play football. I would never play football again. I wanted to block it out, pretend it was not happening. I remember wanting to die. I felt no purpose in being here,' Micilín tells me. His light-blue eyes cloud over slightly. There is more emotion to this young man now, but he still talks as if he is describing someone else's life, someone else's story.

Micilín is full of praise for the National Rehabilitation Hospital. He learned to cope with his physical difficulties, getting regular physiotherapy and speech therapy. He also learned to deal with the emotional impact of an acquired brain injury. 'That's where my social life was resuscitated,' he jokes. 'I made friends, spoke to nurses, other patients, doctors, everyone. That's how I got my confidence back, and how I got the confidence to do public speaking. I took part in a Road Safety Authority television advertisement on the dangers of drink-driving. Rehab helped me achieve things.'

Once discharged, Micilín spent a difficult year at home, listening to his favourite musician – John Beag – and staring at the four walls. Without the support of fellow patients and staff, he found everyday life a challenge, and suffered from

loneliness. He thought it was best to break off his engage-
ment to Caroline. 'I didn't want her to have a life spent
looking after me. I thought I'd be worse than I am now. I
said that we should take a break and we did. I still have her
number and text her from time to time, but she has her own
life now, and I have mine. I knew it wouldn't be fair on her,
and didn't expect her to stand by me.' Micilín moved back
into his mother's house and spent his days wishing for
things to be different.

'The problem was I was a fella who used to wake up
every morning at six-thirty, go out working for the day, and
come home to play sports. I had a busy life. I worked in
Galway mostly, but also Mayo, and Swords in County
Dublin. I loved my Gaelic. I miss football the most. I still
know the lads who play; they are still friends. I miss the
banter in the dressing room, the craic. When I was voted
Player of the Year, my mother had to collect my trophy
because I was in a coma. The players took a vote before the
crash. It was just after the last game I played. I voted for my
friend, who was later killed in a car crash. I was a very
sporty, outgoing person. I was a social creature. I was in
love. I was young and carefree.'

It doesn't matter how much time passes, Micilín can't
forget who he once was. At times, he strikes me as being
acutely aware of all that he has lost. His freedom is limited.
Living in such a remote area, he is dependent on his family
to drive him where he has to go. He is living off disability
allowance from the State and is not in a position to work.
His days are uneventful and isolating. He sits in his
armchair and watches television, or he might call up to a
friend's house for a game of snooker and some beers. Most

of his friends are working during the day. 'It is restricting. I can't drive or work and around here there is nothing really to do. I can't even go walking on a beautiful day like today, as it can be quite tiring. I can't walk very well. It's human nature for me to miss my old life. I think about it a lot.'

Micilín is quick to point out his progress over the past four years. He can feed himself now. He can talk and be understood. He can even remember to turn off the gas, but he will never stop second-guessing himself. 'At the beginning, you couldn't leave me on my own for any length of time. I would leave the gas on and go to light a cigarette. I would forget things so easily. My memory is better, but still not great. With a brain injury, you can never be certain; there is always a nagging at the back of your head if something is fact. If you have a brain injury, you're thinking, oh God, I have a brain injury and I might not get this right.'

The support of his family has helped him immeasurably. He knows it must be difficult for them. 'I could not tell you the exact changes that my siblings have found, but they must have seen a great difference in the brother I was and the one I became. My family have been brilliant. I could not have gone through it without their support. If I'm not feeling great, they give me the space and let me deal with it myself. When they were handing out families, I was blessed.'

Because of his injury, Micilín also suffers from depression. The long days and loneliness, the regret and restrictions can get him down. Just before Christmas 2008, he spent a week in University Hospital Galway, a chance, he says, to recharge his batteries. 'My emotions are all over the place, and can go up and down. They are difficult to control. I can express myself socially, but not emotionally any more.'

Physically, the right-hand side of his body is weakened. He is right-handed, so his writing is very poor. He recently joined Quest, a National Learning Network service in Galway, helping people to rebuild their lives after a brain injury. 'My life changed for the better with Quest. Everyone had suffered brain injuries; everyone was the same. I didn't think I was an outcast.'

Feeling like an outsider is one of the most challenging aspects of having a brain injury. 'People I knew treated me differently at first, but now they've got to know that I'm the same person with far more difficulties than I used to have,' he says. 'Some people would barely speak to me and those who talked to me would only speak about the weather and move on. But now I get told the scandals of the day.'

Meeting new people can prove problematic for Micilín Feeney. 'People don't know how to react to you if you have a brain injury; they're thinking, oh God, he's a mutant. It's the same all over the country, from what people have told me. I want to be the poster child for people with brain injuries. I can be normal . . . well not normal, but then what's normal? I'm not a freak. It can be very disheartening sometimes when stupid people, rather than talk to you, just avoid you because you've got a disability. I have a disability, but it's my disability, not theirs.'

When I ask Micilín how much he understands about what happened to him, he looks me straight in the eye and says, 'I understand I was very stupid and ignorant. My message to people would be to never ever drink and drive and don't judge people just because they are different to you. Most young people are naive and have an "it will never happen to me" attitude. I was like that. I have only recently accepted what has happened to me. Talking to teenagers at schools is a kind of therapy for me. I'm grateful for the talks. It is exciting to meet different people and tell them about my life. It is more than a pastime for me because I've been given the opportunity to save someone from themselves.' It has been an arduous journey for Micilín. Along the way, he encountered many obstacles; each door that shut behind him must have been like a little death.

Micilín lives for the weekends when he goes to the local pub and meets with friends and family. He still enjoys his few pints, although admits that his capacity for drink is far less than it was. He started to drink again a year after his crash and never considered quitting. 'Around here, it's very hard to do anything that does not involve drinking.'

We part company and I drive along the country lane. It meanders like a river. I beep at blind corners for fear of meeting other motorists. I pass the now-closed school Micilín attended as a boy, where he must have played in the yard to the perpetual noise of the ocean – animated and loud – running around and scoring goals. Now, his life has changed forever. He is stuck with his mistake.

6

REMEMBERING KEVIN

'All the rugby games ever played mean much, much less than the life of a single teenage boy.' Vincent Tierney

Barbeque smoke mingles with the mid-August air. I notice that the grass has been recently cut. Inhaling the late summer smell, I watch the volunteer chefs working together, flipping burgers. Kevin's aunt prongs a sausage.

'No, not quite ready yet,' she tells me with a wide smile. Children squeal with delight as the bouncy castle takes shape before them. Older residents sit and chat under the white marquee. The DJ is spinning tunes everybody knows. In the distance, a group of men togged out in red and white football gear move in star shapes up and down the pitch. They are warming up.

'Come on, lads,' shouts a woman wheeling a pushchair. She stands along the touchline. Other excited onlookers stamp their feet in anticipation of a good game. The teams are uneven, but this is the way it has always been. For the past four years, on an August afternoon, a group of teenagers get together to play against a squad of older men in a special game of football. The Kevin Walsh soccer tournament is a tribute to a young footballer who lost his life in a car crash on 1 April 2006, just days after his sixteenth birthday.

The annual event takes place close to Kevin's home, at Bruff Football Club in County Limerick, and kicks off with a novelty game, where Kevin's relations take on his friends. Then local rivals Bruff and Harbertstown battle it out for goals. The winning team walks away with the Kevin Walsh Cup. Kevin's family and Bruff Football Club jointly sponsor the competition.

'He was a totally devoted sportsman, so it's a fitting way to remember him,' says Kate Walsh, Kevin's mother. She is thrilled with the turnout. 'This is the first year it has not rained. There is always a great atmosphere; the whole community comes along. Look at all these people. Kevin deserved this.'

Kevin Walsh played soccer for County Limerick. He was one of the most promising players in the schoolboy league. His manager, Jamsie Carroll, who never misses this event, recalls: 'He came to me when he was fifteen. He was a left-footed player which every team needs. His speed and ball control were impressive. He was my star player, could shoot with both feet, a character, and I saw great potential in him. All the lads loved him.'

Those same lads are here now in a stuffy dressing room. They are no longer schoolboys, but young men of eighteen and nineteen. Some have left for college, others have moved away from Bruff to work, but all have come home for this tournament. Bobby O'Brien was Kevin's best friend. A tall, athletic youth with freckles and floppy hair, he still finds the tragedy difficult to accept. He knows that he and his friends have to move on, but he also believes they need to do that without forgetting Kevin. 'It's nice to remember Kevin. He loved soccer and I suppose this is the one day of the year when we can have a bit of fun while remembering him. It's nearly four years since he died, but it doesn't feel that long. We were all only fifteen when the accident happened. It is strange to see us all growing up. We try to imagine what Kevin would be like now. It was a massive shock to lose him. It was, and still is, hard to believe. We were all so close to him and he was taken so quickly.'

Kevin died instantly when a jeep drove into the back of his family's car. He was a back-seat passenger in the car, which was stopped at the time of the crash. The 4 x 4 vehicle was being driven by former Irish rugby international Eddie Halvey. The sportsman was more than two times over the legal alcohol limit when the crash happened at Coole, near Toomevara, County Tipperary, in 2006. He did not receive a prison sentence when he was convicted for drink-driving and careless driving in May 2009.

On the morning of 1 April 2006, Kevin Walsh set his alarm for 3.45 a.m. It was an early start, but he knew the trip to Northern Ireland with his two favourite uncles would be worth dragging himself out of his warm bed for. He quickly got dressed, grabbed his coat and popped his iPod in his jeans pocket. His uncle and godfather, 30-year-old Vincent Tierney, pulled up outside in his BMW. His other uncle, 37-year-old Declan Tierney was in the passenger seat. Kevin saw the lights from the car and quietly left the house, careful not to wake his mother, Kate, or his sister, Mandy. He settled himself into the back seat, excited about the prospect of helping his uncles choose a new motor. They were going to Newry to view cars for Declan's hackney business. His uncles never went to a motor showroom without Kevin, knowing how much he loved cars. If they dared, they would never hear the end of it.

'Sit back there now, small man, and get some sleep. You'll want to be awake to spot the women on the way back home,' Vincent said. Kevin took his advice and started to doze. Declan, too, closed his eyes. Shortly before 5 a.m., Vincent noticed some movement up ahead. Slowing down, he saw that the dark shapes obstructing the N7 Limerick to Dublin road were cattle. He managed to drive cautiously around the animals, before pulling into the hard shoulder. He put on his hazard lights and flashed at a lorry that was approaching him from the Dublin side. The truck driver slowed down and crawled past them. Declan then rang the gardaí in Roscrea to report the obstruction. It was a pitch-dark morning. They were concerned for other motorists. Kevin woke up, still wearing his seat belt, and leaned towards his uncles.

'It's only cattle on the road. Go back to sleep, young man,' Vincent said. Moments later, Vincent heard a car coming from behind. He remembers that it sounded louder than it should. *Why has that not passed me by now?* he thought. Glancing in his rear view mirror, he saw that the bright lights of the 4 x 4 jeep were directly behind him.

'Jesus!' he roared as he moved to release the handbrake.

He got no further. The 2005 registered Toyota Landcruiser struck the rear of his BMW. At 5.10 a.m., gardaí came across the two-vehicle collision. Vincent had blacked out. When he came to, Declan was calling Kevin. There was no response from the back seat. Vincent reached back to try to rouse his nephew, but he could not. He opened the driver's door and got out. Leaning against the side of the car, he saw blue lights flashing. Was Kevin still alive? Had he just imagined that his godson was dead? The thought that he might not live was too much to take. He could feel blood trickling down his face. The taste was sour. His head had smashed the windscreen with the force of the impact. After a few minutes, a garda guided him into the back of an ambulance. 'Just make sure there is someone with Kevin,' Vincent said.

Declan Tierney was trapped in the passenger seat. A searing pain ripped down his spine. Immediately after the crash, he looked back towards Kevin. He reached for his hand and searched his young face for an expression. There was nothing – no pulse or sign of life. He knew Kevin was gone. The iPod in his jeans pocket was crushed. Declan shouted, 'The child, the child!' A fire officer on the scene got into the back seat. He rested Kevin's head on his lap. He placed one hand on Declan's shoulder and said, 'I have him now; I'll mind him.' Those few words of comfort meant everything in that moment.

Detective Garda Declan O'Carroll, who was also present, tried to revive Kevin but was unable to do so. At this stage, Eddie Halvey was on the side of the road. He was unsteady on his feet and appeared to be drunk. Declan Tierney was eventually cut free from the wreckage. Both the

Tierney brothers were taken by ambulance to Nenagh General Hospital. Declan was lying on a stretcher when his mobile phone rang. It was a garda in Roscrea station asking if the problem with the cattle had been sorted out.

The body of Kevin Walsh was taken to Nenagh General Hospital in a second ambulance. At his home in Bruff, there was a loud banging on the front door. His mother, Kate, jumped out of her bed and ran to the curtains. She opened the window to find her brother, Monty Tierney, in the driveway. He was distressed and asked her to come with him.

'The lads have had a bit of an accident,' he said.

'What lads?' Kate asked.

'Declan and Vincent,' he said.

'Kevin is gone,' Kate said.

'What are you talking about? He has hurt his hand,' said Monty. But Kate knew that her only son, the younger of her two children, would have texted her to say he was okay. She knew before being told that he was dead.

Kate arrived at Nenagh General Hospital just as the two ambulances were pulling in. Frantic, she dashed towards the back of the ambulance carrying Kevin. She had one thing on her mind: she had to see her baby boy. Banging on the doors of the ambulance, Kate started to cry uncontrollably. A garda approached her, gently putting his arms around her. 'You don't have to see this,' he said, coaxing her away from the doors. Kate's brothers were then brought into the emergency department.

'I saw Vincent covered in blood and Declan attached to an oxygen apparatus. I thought to myself: if they are this bad, what does Kevin look like?' she recalls. As Kate waited in the emergency department, a doctor pronounced Kevin dead in the ambulance. Monty Tierney identified the sixteen-year-old as his nephew. Kate was then taken to a small chapel at the back of the hospital, where Kevin was laid out on the stretcher. She remembers thinking that his neck was severely swollen. She touched his forehead and called out to him. 'It was the first time in my life that he never answered me,' she says.

Kevin Walsh had suffered severe internal injuries. He had bruising to his chest from the safety belt and some slight bruising to his face.

Following a post mortem examination, Kevin's family were permitted to take him home one last time. 'I brought him home on Sunday and kept him until Tuesday morning in our house. I slept with him on the last night. I put my face against his face in his coffin and I stayed with him all night. We closed the kitchen doors. It was just the two of us, mother and son. Nobody interfered. I held onto his hands that were black with bruising. The family left me on my own that last night; the way I wanted it to be.'

A song interrupts our conversation. The pitch erupts in melody and Kate excuses herself to walk towards the middle of the football field. Kevin's friends and family are linking arms, swaying now and singing along to 'You'll Never Walk Alone.' Every year, the Liverpool football team's anthem prompts the same reaction, grown men holding on to each other, fighting back tears, singing their hearts out. Kevin's friends, too, bellow out the tune, making space for Kate as she joins the circle. The DJ is clapping his hands above the decks. Seated supporters are standing. The sky overhead is a pale blue, with sporadic streaks of violet, but no threat of rain. I notice Kate leaving the group before the end of the song. She jogs towards the top corner of the pitch, alone. Afterwards she tells me that she had to take a moment.

'If they see me upset, they get upset and I don't want that on today of all days. Kevin was an avid Liverpool supporter. He was due to go to Anfield with his dad, Jim, to see his heroes play. It was his sixteenth birthday present. Jim and I are separated, but Kevin has a good relationship with his dad. They were going to fly over to Liverpool in mid-April, two weeks after his birthday, but he was killed before he got the chance.'

Kate Walsh finds it difficult to accept that the person responsible for Kevin's death escaped a jail term. Thirty-eight-year-old Eddie Halvey did not even face the charge of dangerous driving causing death. The former Munster and Ireland rugby player was arrested at the scene of the fatal collision and subsequent breath tests showed there was an alcohol concentration of 83 mg of alcohol per 100 ml of breath. The legal limit at the time was 35 mg per 100 ml of breath. It took three long years for the case to come before the court.

In January 2008, Kate Walsh learned that the case might never get a hearing. Owing to difficulties with the forensic evidence and other factors in establishing the exact cause of the collision, the Director of Public Prosecutions decided to drop the charge of dangerous driving causing death against Eddie Halvey. At the time, the Walsh family was not told why the charge was withdrawn. A distraught Kate was determined to get her day in court. She hired a private investigator to look into the circumstances surrounding the crash. She also began a nationwide petition urging the Director of Public Prosecutions to reverse the decision, and collected more than 20,000 signatures.

In July 2008, in a dramatic turnaround by the Director of Public Prosecutions, it was decided that Eddie Halvey would face charges in relation to the death of Kevin Walsh. The DPP accepted the lesser charge of careless driving.

After three years of legal drama, on 12 May 2009, at a sitting of Nenagh Circuit Court, Eddie Halvey finally faced trial in connection with Kevin Walsh's death. He pleaded guilty to careless driving and to drink-driving.

It was a day with the promise of summer, the sunlight bouncing off the grey stone courthouse. A small group of media was in place inside the black railings, TV crews and photographers. Kevin Walsh's family sat together in court, unified in their shared grief and expectation of justice. Kate Walsh wore black. Outside, she smoked nervously, surrounded by her brothers and her only surviving child, 23-year-old Mandy. The family had come to court hoping for something other than what they got.

Following an emotional hearing, Judge Tom Teehan gave Eddie Halvey a seven-month suspended prison sentence and banned him from driving for seven years. He also ordered him to keep the peace and be of good behaviour for five years. Defence barrister Patrick Gageby provided the judge with medical reports concerning Eddie Halvey. They found that he had become introverted and had been prescribed antidepressant medication following the crash. He had also received counselling for his depression.

In court, former rugby colleagues, there to support him, surrounded Eddie Halvey. Irish sporting hero Mick Galwey was by his side. He took the stand to speak on the defendant's behalf and gave evidence as to how his former teammate had been a different man since the crash and felt much remorse. 'At times I worry about him. He had a great circle of friends and was well thought of, but he left Limerick and moved to Dublin. His confidence is gone.'

Kate Walsh, unimpressed by this evidence, took the stand to read her victim impact statement. Composed and determined, she told the court that Eddie Halvey had robbed her of a lifetime with Kevin. She said she still buys her son the latest Liverpool jersey when it comes out and puts it on his grave. 'I couldn't believe that it was someone else's stupidity that killed Kevin, someone who had chosen to drive after having drink taken. He didn't have to die; he was only a child sitting in the back of a stopped car. Kevin had always said that he would be a star and, thanks to Eddie Halvey, he is, but for all the wrong reasons.' Kate Walsh then turned towards Eddie Halvey and told him that she will never forgive or forget him for his ignorance and selfishness and for killing her son.

In his evidence, Eddie Halvey, an imposing, well-groomed figure, said that Mrs Walsh had every right to feel the way she did. He said that he would have to live with the shame of what he had done for the rest of his life. He then looked directly towards her in the public gallery and said, 'I am truly sorry for what I have done to you and your family and I don't expect forgiveness. I really don't.'

Kate believes this apology was too little too late. 'Only for the judge that day, Eddie Halvey would never have apologised,' she says. 'I can't ever see myself forgiving him. If he had come to me a week or two after Kevin's funeral and said "I'm sorry", it might have been different. Even if he had sent a bunch of flowers, but there was nothing from him for years. He only apologised when he had to.'

Speaking after the sentencing, Kate told the waiting press that the wrong message had been sent to the rest of the country. 'I am very bitter with the justice system in this country,' she said. 'I feel very bitter towards Eddie Halvey. He is a sportsman who played for Ireland and he got a slap on the wrist for killing my son. Go out, play sports for Ireland, drink-drive, you can kill someone and you won't get punished in court for it. That is the reality. We are disappointed.'

Four months later, she shares the same sentiments with me. 'I feel our justice system failed us; it let us down. I honestly thought that man would go to jail. He killed a child. He was over the limit. There were three adults there on the night of the crash. My two brothers, Vincent and Declan, were sober, and the man who was over the limit, his word was taken in court instead. We waited three years for justice that never came. If he was an ordinary Joe Soap, he would be in prison by now and it would not have taken three years to put him there either. There have been similar collisions around this area involving young lads and drinking, and those lads are serving time for what they did. I believe that Eddie Halvey walked because of who he was and because of his status in society. I wanted justice but I got nothing and I lost a beautiful son.'

Kate lifts up the arm of her T-shirt to reveal an ink tattoo of Kevin's face. It is her only tattoo, which she had done especially for Kevin's eighteenth birthday. 'He used to always say he would get a tattoo when he turned eighteen. I would tell him not while you are living under my roof. It was a running joke between us. I don't even like tattoos, but I did this for him. He was a fabulous son. I always say he was too good for this world. Kevin put others first. He would put on my electric blanket before I went to bed, or he would have a cup of tea waiting for me when I'd come in from work. He was so thoughtful and would have made some lucky girl a great husband one day.'

Vincent Tierney, the driver of the car and Kevin's godfather, will never see Kevin marry, get his Leaving Certificate or drive his first car. He lives with the guilt of this every single day. 'I carry the pain of knowing that I took him and therefore I should have looked after him, and made sure nothing happened to him. Every day, I think of it and every night I pray to Kevin to keep me sane, to keep me from going mad.' Vincent and Kevin were inseparable. 'We had a very close relationship. He was as good as my own and that still hurts.' They shared an interest in cars and sport. The week before he died, Vincent bought Kevin a new car. 'He would have had to wait for his seventeenth birthday to drive it, but it needed some work and he could have spent the year getting it ready,' he explains. The car takes pride of place at this tournament, on show by the main gates to Bruff Football Club. The green and black bonnet is sparkling, the leather interior spotless.

'This is the main event of the year for us as a family. This is our Christmas. We look forward to it every year. I bring Kevin's car to put on display here for everyone to see. I drive it once a year for a week on his anniversary. This tournament shows how important Kevin was, how much he was loved and is still loved,' Vincent Tierney says.

At his house, near Bruff, Vincent has converted a garage into a shrine for Kevin. The small space is bright; the main colours are red and white. A snooker table sits in the middle of the floor, where Kevin's friends can come and play. Liverpool memorabilia adorn the walls, a signed jersey, a football and posters. There are photographs of Kevin at his best, playing football, scoring goals, smiling with his teammates. A framed picture of two men in suits, standing tall, wide smiles, hangs beside a pair of hurling sticks. It shows an uncle with his nephew, and was taken on Vincent's wedding day, when Kevin was a groomsman.

Just a few months later, Vincent was talking to Kevin in a hospital morgue, when he approached him to say that he was sorry, that he should have left him at home. For months after his death, Vincent refused to have any children. Newly married, his relationship was under serious strain. He took the decision to go to counselling, which he still attends. He was prescribed the anti-anxiety drug Zanex and still takes the medication. Kevin is buried just outside Bruff, a mile from Vincent's house. Every evening for a year, he visited the cemetery because it was where he felt comfortable. Two and a half years after the crash, he had a son of his own, Ross Kevin. 'We thought about calling him Kevin, but my heart would not have been able to handle that. I think there is a bit of Kevin that came back with him. I have to keep strong now for my son. He has just had his first birthday. Kate and Mandy are crazy about him, which eases my pain.'

Vincent often thinks back to the night of the crash and the subsequent court case. 'We were there that night. We did everything right and we paid the ultimate price. I understand Eddie Halvey went out drinking. He did not intentionally go out to kill anyone. He didn't decide to drive into the back of a parked car and kill a young boy. But why didn't he be a man about it and admit it? That would have been enough. Unlike Kate, I don't think he should have gone to prison. In my opinion, putting the man in jail would have served no purpose. I think the family would have been a lot more grateful with an apology, and not inside in a court, not in front of a judge.'

Vincent's baby boy is looking for him. He shuffles up to him with a broad smile and points towards the barbeque. We join the line. Kevin's friends are queuing for hot dogs. They've worked up an appetite after the game and are looking forward to the food. 'Not having him around is the hardest thing; he was great craic,' they tell me. 'When he was taken from us, it took something away from everyone.'

At the next table, Kate is serving tea from a large aluminium pot. She smiles at the young men, knowing that they will call around to her house to watch the upcoming Champions League games, to share in the highs and lows of Liverpool's performance. She will offer them cans of beer, crisps and sausage rolls. They will fill her sitting room with laughter and chat, and she is grateful that, even though he is gone, Kevin still has his friends.

7

PEDESTRIAN BEWARE!

'I saw the Sergeant, a Guard and a priest. The minute I saw the priest, I knew James was dead. I knew he hadn't been injured. I knew he was dead.' Jim Nash

James Nash had been warned – 'Never walk home alone at night' – but, like many teenagers, he chose to ignore this advice. The trainee chef was young and carefree. He saw no reason to fear walking along the familiar roads where he had grown up, the streets close to his home in Kilworth, County Cork. Taking risks involved the unfamiliar – bungee jumping or racing cars. Sauntering home in the dead of night after a few pints with friends was no threat.

James lived with his parents, Jim and Kay Nash, in a secluded bungalow on an acre of land off a quiet country lane. He enjoyed socialising in the nearby towns of Fermoy and Mitchelstown. The secondary roads home were poorly lit, winding and dangerous. James knew the twists and turns, the sharp corners and straight stretches. He could see the lights of approaching cars long before they could see him. His parents just worried unnecessarily and taxis were often in short supply.

One evening, after a Friday night out in Mitchelstown, he decided to walk the five miles home. Jim and Kay Nash were waiting up for him. Kay checked the curtains every time she saw the lights of a car in the distance. She knew she shouldn't worry. But was he old enough to be trusted? Eventually, just as *The Late Late Show* came to a close, they heard the key turn in the lock. Kay breathed a sigh of relief before inquiring how James had got home. His face was flushed, his cheeks red and eyes moist. It was pitch dark outside. He told his parents he had walked back from town. Jim and Kay were furious with him.

The following morning, Kay woke James early. He might have had a slight hangover but she didn't care. She was determined to teach him a lesson. It would be for his own good, and might even save him from himself. She told him to get into the car; they were going for a drive. Taking the same route he had walked the previous night, Kay pointed out a number of small plaques at various locations along the stretch of road. Each plaque was a memorial, commemorating individuals who had been knocked down and killed on that road.

'Don't ever walk home again, not on this road, it is lethal. Always ring home. No matter what time of the day or night, you'll be picked up. I don't want you to become another statistic,' Kay told her son.

A year after that conversation, at the tender age of nineteen, James Nash became another statistic. He now has his own plaque, just outside Fermoy, three miles from the family home. On a small piece of limestone, the simple inscription reads, 'James, 2000.' The monument marks the place where he was knocked down by a bread lorry.

Nine years on, his father, sixty-year-old Jim, who has recently retired from agricultural research work in Teagasc, keeps the area around the headstone tidy. He cuts the grass and picks up any rubbish. He chose the rectangular piece of limestone. It was important that something marked the spot, but he wanted to ensure that it was subtle, understated, a gentle reminder of a life lost.

Jim also looks after the upkeep of his only son's grave in Kilworth churchyard. He has adopted the role of caretaker; the work he has done and continues to do here is a labour of love.

Kilworth makes a good first impression, with its neat hedgerows, colourful flowerpots and charming village green. Facing the green is an old Protestant church with a graveyard, used by both Catholics and Protestants.

'Ten years ago, it was impossible to tell that this was a graveyard,' Jim says. 'The entire place was a wilderness – overgrown, unkempt and thick with weeds. We had to trample down to our family plot on a makeshift path for James's burial in February 2000.'

Since then, Jim Nash has transformed the churchyard into the serene setting it is today. Every evening after work, he travelled to the cemetery to mow, slash, plant and rake. A keen gardener, Jim considered the project cathartic. 'It was a kind of therapy for me. As the cemetery began to take shape, I was proud of what I was achieving and I was doing this for my son.'

Behind the high stone walls, amid the narrow pebble-stone paths, lined with traditional yew trees, Jim tends to the public herb garden he has planted. A delicious fusion of scents emanates from the collection of plants. 'Locals can come and take what they need. There is mint, rosemary, basil, fennel and parsley. James loved to cook and these herbs enhance our food. People sometimes just come to sit on the wooden benches and relax in the quiet. This is an oasis of calm, fitting for my dead son and for the village of Kilworth.'

James Nash was a popular local lad, who did his best to please people. At the time of his death, he was on a FÁS chef training course in Cork, and getting work experience in the Grand Hotel in Fermoy. When a colleague of his asked him to a Debs ball in Fermoy, he was flattered and agreed to go. The event was to be held on Friday 5 February 2000 in the hotel where the pair worked. Having just finished a week of long shifts, James was extremely tired. In truth, he was not really in the mood for a ball, but felt obliged to attend. Earlier that day, he had asked his father if he could borrow a pair of black shoes. His trendy runners and brown brogues would not be smart enough for the black-tie event. When he got home, James found that his father had polished the shoes and left them out for him. Checking himself in the full-length mirror, James was pleased with his smart appearance. 'I could tell he was happy with how he looked. He grabbed his wallet and packet of cigarettes before leaving for the Grand Hotel. He made sure to put five pounds into his cigarette box,' says Jim.

Coincidentally, Jim Nash, a fiddle player, was taking part in a traditional music session in the Grand Hotel that same night. On three occasions, he went looking for James, but each time he just missed him. When the session ended at around 12.30 a.m., Jim did one final search for James. Scanning the room, he saw no sign of his son, so decided to head home. The place was packed with young people dancing, chatting and singing. He knew James would be having fun by now and would probably not be looking for a lift this early.

Two hours later, James decided to leave for home. The tiredness had finally caught up with him. Exhausted after the long week of work and dancing the night away, he left his work colleague and friends in search of a taxi. Checking his cigarette packet, he made sure the £5 note was still in place. It was. He would need this to get his taxi home. At the taxi rank, James discovered that he would have to queue for at least an hour before getting a cab. It was a dry night after a day of heavy rain. James just wanted his bed. He decided he would be quicker walking out the road. He had left his new mobile phone at home, otherwise he would possibly have called his parents. Making his way towards the outskirts of the town, he passed a phone box. The words of his mother Kay might have rang in his ears. 'Always phone. Don't walk home on your own, any time of the day or night.' James probably checked the time. It was after 2.30 a.m. Jim believes that James did not want to bother them. 'He was a grown man and the last thing he wanted was to wake his parents at that hour of night. I'm sure he thought that mothers could be over-protective. I imagine he picked up the pace, bracing himself against the cold night air,' Jim says.

It was a quiet night. James, who was dressed in dark clothing, was careful to keep close to the edge of the road.

He had already walked a mile when he heard the sound of a truck approaching from behind. In the harsh lights of the truck, he could see a large pool of water stretching out from the ditch to the yellow line in front of him. Jim Nash believes that James then stepped out to avoid getting wet, but misjudged the distance between himself and the passing truck.

The driver of the 45-foot-long bread lorry did not see the figure step into his path. He was not expecting anybody to be out walking in the middle of the night. It was not even clear he had hit someone.

James died instantly. The doctor who examined him at the scene assured the Nash family that he had not felt a thing, that he probably did not even know he had been hit. James had struck the road immediately. The truck drove over him but its wheels did not touch his body.

Jim Nash is grateful that the family were able to have an open coffin. 'With many road crash victims, families can't have an open coffin. We are grateful that we could say goodbye to his face. He suffered severe head and chest injuries as well as a broken ankle. The road killed him, in the end.'

That night, the doorbell in the Nash house rang at 3.30 a.m. Jim was relieved. 'At least now he's home,' he told his wife, 'we can have a proper sleep. He must have forgotten his keys.' Kay got out of bed to let James in. Moments later, she came back into the bedroom to say that the gardaí were at the door. Jim immediately thought of the trouble James might be in. Had he got into a row? Was he sitting in the back of the squad car? Did they have to drive him home? He quickly got dressed. When he got to the front door, he froze. It was not the sight of the gardaí that caused his heart to stop fleetingly, but the priest who stood alongside them in the porch.

'I saw the Sergeant, a Guard and a priest. The minute I saw the priest, I knew James was dead. I knew he hadn't been injured. I knew he was dead.'

The gardaí did their duty, asked if this was the Nash family home and if they could come in. One phrase ran through Jim's head incessantly, 'James is dead.' He didn't answer the questions that were being asked. He just kept saying that his son was dead. When it was confirmed, he wanted to know how the three men were so sure. The gardaí told Jim that they had found his son's wallet and a packet of cigarettes, with a folded up £5 note inside them – his unspent taxi fare.

Jim Nash was brought to Cork University Hospital by patrol car. He requested that they stop at the scene of the incident on the N8 main Dublin to Cork road. The truck driver was still there. Jim approached him and shook his hand. 'I know that if you could have avoided it, you would have, because people don't go out to kill people,' he told the driver.

James Nash was brought home for a traditional wake. His older sister, 21-year-old Frances, flew back from college in France for the funeral. At Cork Airport, she asked her father to tell her it was not true. Jim said, 'I would give my soul for it not to be true.'

'Instead of bringing him to a funeral home, we brought him home,' Jim recalls. 'Looking back, it was the best thing for us to have done at the time as it allowed us to come to terms with his death in our own house. I would go down, rub his head, take his hands, talk to him and there was never a sound.'

When the weeks passed and the crowds of mourners went back to their own lives, one memory stood out for the Nash family: it was a case of the kindness of strangers. A couple had made a two-hour journey from Kerry to attend James's wake. The husband and wife approached Jim and Kay and introduced themselves. 'You don't know us at all,' said the man. 'We are strangers to you, but we heard about the accident and we had to visit you because twelve years ago our nineteen-year-old son was also killed in an accident.' They stayed for an hour, drank tea and talked to the Nash family. Before leaving, the man said: 'I'm going to say something to you now and it's not going to make any sense to you, but in the weeks and months ahead when the initial shock of this subsides, do everything that you did every day, because it is the only thing that will make sense of your life from now on.'

Jim often thinks back to this advice. At first, he didn't take much heed. Nothing could ever be considered normal again: gardening or going out for a meal or cooking dinner. His home was a strange place to him. He was waiting for something to happen. He would spend many nights looking into his son's bedroom. The door ajar, he would switch on the light and stare at the empty bed, at James' things, how he had left them. 'The crazy thing was I knew he was never going to be there again. It seemed so unreal,' he recalls. 'It still seems unreal today.'

Gradually Jim moved on, doing his best not to break routines, returning to work at Teagasc. 'People were slightly cagey around me. They didn't know what to say to me. One man passed a strange comment. He said, "You're the last Nash now in Kilworth." I found that a very odd thing to say. Family name obviously meant a lot to him.'

Jim also took up vegetable gardening again, and tackled the challenge of renovating the old cemetery. 'In the first couple of months, you get used to dealing with the stark reality of the immediate loss, when you know that he is not going to walk in, but the pain of the realisation that you are not going to see him again this side of the grave gets stronger with each passing year because the absence is getting longer. In that way, grief gets worse, but there are things you do to help you cope. For me, it's looking after the cemetery.'

When Jim is asked how many children are in his family, he automatically says two. Likewise, when Frances is asked if she has any siblings, she always says that she has one brother. 'I tell people, Frances is working in Law and James was killed in an accident. People can get embarrassed, but I put them at ease by explaining that I have come to terms with his death and don't mind talking about him.' Jim is a different person now to the man he was before he lost his only son. The shift in perspective has altered the way he looks at the world.

'The person I was before James died, that person is gone. My outlook is different. Things that once bothered me don't any more. There are now few things that I would consider important, because I found out the hard way that the only things that are important are your family, your health and the health of your family. Anything else you can get over. I find myself getting amused at the antics of people, who get so tied up with things that have no consequence. If there is a local tragedy, I make a point of being there if I can, if I'm wanted. Our door is always open. Grief is unique, pain is unique, but we can all share in it to ease the burden. When I hear about another road tragedy on the news, I feel sympathy for those families because I know that they have started into a life sentence. They have to face up to it, live with it. I would advise people to have a wake at home, to be around people. I know from my own experience there is nothing people can say. There is no need to say anything. Just being there is enough.'

Jim recalls one priest who came to the house at the time of James' funeral. He believes that he was trying to offer words of comfort, but he failed to inspire anything but anger in James. 'He told me God needed James more than we did, and I told him that that was a load of horse manure. I told him that God has all eternity and said that the next sixty years would not have mattered to him.'

Jim is no longer bitter about his son's death. He doesn't see the point. 'It could have happened to the person next door. It didn't. It happened to me,' he says. 'I lost a wonderful son. Like all teenagers, James could be awkward, between the ages of fifteen and seventeen. He thought he knew it all, but was beginning to realise that he didn't. He was changing rapidly. He had been studying Business in Waterford Institute of Technology, but informed us that he wanted to be a chef. He had no problem pulling out the pan at three o'clock in the morning. He was cautious about telling us, but we were delighted for him. He was beginning to see that, as far as we were concerned, he was free to follow his own career path. As long as he was happy doing what he chose, we were happy. He was really enjoying the cooking. James was a rogue, a mimic, a man with a great sense of sarcasm and wit. We were trying to get him off the cigarettes, but he never got around to quitting.'

Does Jim think that alcohol was the cause of his son's death? He certainly accepts that it was a factor. The inquest into his death found that James Nash had a concentration of 200 mg of alcohol per 100 ml of blood when he was killed. Jim also believes that his son was dressed inappropriately for walking at night. 'There are lessons to be learned from my son's death. The importance of high-visibility jackets should not be underestimated, especially for those walking along main roads with no footpaths. The traffic corps recommends that even if you are out walking in the middle of the day, you should wear some form of high-visibility clothing. It makes sense to be seen. James was not seen. I understand that if someone is going out for the night, they don't want to bring a high-visibility jacket in their pocket, but if they are going to walk home, it's an idea to ask the barman if you can borrow a jacket. But young men don't think about being seen. They think they can't be killed. That is the saddest thing.'

Jim Nash enjoys going for a pint in the evenings in the village of Kilworth. Before he takes his seat at the bar, he always pays a visit to the cemetery, where he chats briefly to James, telling him about his day, letting him know how much he is still loved and missed.

There are times when Jim feels that he could have been dealt a better hand of cards. 'When I was sixteen years old, my father died. He never got to impart his wisdom, advice and commonsense to me. I always said I would do my level best to stay alive to be there for my children, to be there for my son and be able to dispense advice over a shared drink. But James and I can't ever sit at the bar and chat, father to son,' says James. 'I have to chat at his graveside instead. Even now, nine years later, I still find it difficult to believe that he is actually dead, because he shouldn't be.'

The Road Safety Authority (RSA) is continually working on campaigns to make the road a safer place for pedestrians and cyclists. In September 2009, the organisation distributed 40,000 high-visibility vests at the National Ploughing Championships in Athy, County Kildare. RSA Chief Executive Noel Brett, speaking at the launch said, 'This year, we will again be giving out high-visibility vests for adults and children to ensure pedestrians and cyclists are safe on the roads. As the evenings get darker, we can't stress how important it is to be safe and be seen on the road. Wearing a simple high-visibility vest will reduce the risk of being involved in a fatal or serious injury collision. The best advice that we can give is to be aware of your vulnerability on the road, take responsibility for your safety and make sure that everyone in your household wears a high-visibility vest when walking or cycling, day or night. It could be the difference between being seriously injured, killed or living. Quite simply, wearing the vest could save your life.'

In a joint initiative with Age Action Ireland and the Irish Pharmacy Union, the RSA also distributed 200,000 high-visibility jackets for older people in the summer of 2009. Elderly people were encouraged to pick up the free vests at their local chemists. The campaign was designed to improve safety in rural and urban areas and to educate vulnerable road-users of the need to be seen in order to be safe on Irish roads.

As part of its road safety strategy 2007–12, the RSA has highlighted the use of high-visibility material for pedestrians, cyclists and motorcyclists and aims to promote continuous awareness of their importance for vulnerable road users.

While young men aged seventeen to thirty-four are consistently over-represented in collisions, fatality and serious injury statistics, older men are also significantly at risk, particularly as pedestrians. Older people are the group most at risk when walking on Irish roads. The RSA has found that male pensioners are three times more likely than other pedestrians to be killed while walking on Irish roads and female pensioners are twice as likely to be killed. They are more vulnerable when they are hit by a vehicle than other pedestrians, and are more likely to die or to be disabled by severe injury. When hospitalised, their length of stay is much longer than that of younger people.

Road crash data shows that 2003 had one of the lowest recorded numbers of pedestrian deaths, at sixty-three. This corresponded with the introduction of penalty points for speeding offences, making pedestrians the road-user group that most benefited from the initial introduction of the system.

8

CHANGED LIVES

'. . . no matter how long you spend in a hospital like this, you are not going to get better. That is the real nub of severe disability.' Dr Mark Delargy, National Rehabilitation Hospital.

I t is like any other children's hospital ward, with cartoon characters on the wall, toy boxes and teddy bears, except that half the children are road-crash victims. Their recuperation could take longer, and some may never fully recover. Learning to adapt to a new way of life because of a spinal or brain injury can take years: for many, it is back to basics: how to get dressed, go the toilet, or even walk and talk. A ten-year-old boy, who lost an arm, bounces a basketball diligently, eyes focused, a streak of sheer determination across his brow. Later, he will show off this newly acquired skill in the children's gym downstairs.

The National Rehabilitation Hospital is a place of untold stories, where hundreds of people come to rebuild shattered lives every year. The Dun Laoghaire facility is the only dedicated rehabilitation unit in the country, dealing with brain and spinal cord injuries as well as patients with prosthetic limbs.

At any one time, up to 50 per cent of patients in the hospital have been admitted because of road traffic collisions. For every death on Irish roads, it is estimated that eight people are seriously injured. The National Rehabilitation Hospital treats the majority of those people, the survivors of road crashes.

The car park has more disabled spaces than other hospitals. A couple manoeuvre themselves from their car into wheelchairs, and get what they need from the vehicle's boot. A man walks by; they ask him to shut the boot and he obliges. The man in the wheelchair has a bitter look on his face that he cannot shake off. He wears a pair of fingerless gloves, probably to protect his hands from the constant friction of his palms against the wheel. His female partner follows him into the hospital, where they possibly met, and now visit as outpatients.

In the lobby, a young woman is sitting, reading a magazine. She looks perfectly healthy. It is only when she starts to move that her injury becomes apparent; she shuffles down the corridor, shoulders jerking as she struggles to maintain her balance. The human traffic in the high-ceilinged hallways is slow-moving. The noticeboards advertise swivel seats and stair lifts. There are no signs for oncology or emergency. Instead, the chapel and the library are clearly marked.

Forty of the hospital's 119 beds are for brain-damaged patients. A quarter of all patients in the brain injury unit are young men who were involved in road traffic collisions. Acquired brain injury is a highly complex condition, with devastating effects for the patient, but also, and sometimes even more so, for the family of the injured person.

St Patrick's Ward caters for patients with severe brain damage and behavioural difficulties. The doors are kept locked. Beside each bed is a whiteboard. Every day, the nurses write down important pieces of information for each patient – things like, 'Hi Seán, today is Monday, 17th August 2009'. There are also a number of lockers, like those found in secondary school corridors, with the names of the patients clearly pinned to the metal doors. Those who come to St Patrick's stay for a term of at least three months and they need the closet space.

Dr Mark Delargy spends his working life trying to fix broken people. As director of the national brain injury service, he treats survivors of road crashes. His job is to try to salvage as much as possible of the pre-crash personality and skills of these severely injured people. 'The statistics for road deaths has a multiplier for survivors who suffer sufficient trauma to disrupt their lives, sometimes entirely reversible, such as broken bones. At the other end of the spectrum is brain injury,' Dr Delargy says.

All too often, because of the nature of car crashes and the speeds involved, brain injury is a major factor. Victims are rushed to the neurology departments at Beaumont Hospital in Dublin or Cork University Hospital, where life-saving surgery is carried out. Blood clots may be removed. Families are told that there is a fifty-fifty survival rate. Every minute counts. Some patients survive, but can be left with lasting damage to the brain.

'The most extreme form of brain injury is the vegetative state, where the person awakes but is unaware of and unresponsive to the world or to stimuli such as pain,' Dr Delargy explains. 'He/she will never move normally again, remain essentially wheelchair-dependent, and never talk or walk or communicate in any useful fashion. The grades of recovery transfer to difficulties with walking, communicating, thinking and personality. When brain scans show that there are still problems, the neurosurgeons refer patients to the National Rehabilitation Hospital, where the hard work begins for both patients and their families.'

The road to recovery is different for each patient, depending on the part of the brain that has been damaged. The hospital takes a multidisciplinary approach to treatment. The team of medical professionals reflects the various functions of the brain: speech, thinking, personality, coordination and balance. For example, the brain helps you to walk and talk, so speech therapists and physiotherapists form part of the rehabilitation team; occupational therapists work on life skills, how we look after ourselves in daily living; nursing teams take care of problems with continence and nutrition; and the doctors look at thinking, personality and changed behaviour.

'My work focuses on behavioural changes after a traumatic brain injury, where there has been damage to the frontal lobes of the brain, the part that houses our personality, judgement and executive decision-making skills,' says Dr Delargy. 'The crux of a brain injury is that you are using the damaged organ to monitor your own progress. If you have an impaired mechanism for analysing your own performance, then you will come up with the wrong answers.

You think you are better than you are. You misjudge your interactions with other people, your ability to carry out certain tasks. You assume there is no problem, because your brain is not telling you there is a problem. The lack of insight is rather like being drunk. How do you guide someone if they are telling you that they don't have those injuries?'

Telling patients that they have a problem is not enough. The medical team has to demonstrate through a real-life scenario that the patient's skills have been compromised. A simple task is set, such as sorting out a box of different-coloured objects within a certain time-frame. Before the task, patients agree that the task is perfectly straightforward and one they will be able to perform without difficulty. After the exercise, their performance is measured and discussed. When the patient is told that he or she took far longer than international norms to complete the task, they find this difficult to accept, and often justify their slow performance with excuses, as Dr Delargy explains: 'They try to validate their own self-belief system because their core structure says I should be able to do that, so they find a reason why the task was invalid for them.'

Doctors, then, when dealing with brain injury patients can encounter daily battles. Rather than argue with patients, they have to reset various tasks in a different way so that eventually patients become more likely to accept the results as valid.

'Some people make a good physical recovery, but are unable to accept changes in their performance, interaction with others and their social abilities. They have considerable difficulties with interpersonal relationships and may never return to work. Generally, they fall out with all manner of people,' says Dr Delargy. This is particularly hard on families. 'These patients live life as different people, often very difficult people who have issues with aggression. Our personality is down to nerve interconnectivity and transmitter function in our frontal lobe, as well as our conditioning and value systems. Once you surgically remove somebody's frontal lobe, like a lobotomy, you are a changed person. By the nature of trauma to the brain, patients have what we call a partial lobotomy and the changes can be equally devastating.

'It is well understood that if a certain area of the brain is affected, we may not speak properly again, as in the case of many stroke victims. If our personality centre is affected, then the equivalent of losing the ability to speak from a very severe stroke can be mirrored in a frontal lobe brain injury, where the personality is radically different. And no matter how long you spend in a hospital like this, you are not going to get better. That is the real nub of severe disability.'

Patients come into the National Rehabilitation Hospital with an agenda – for example, that they want to walk again, a target that, for many, is never going to be achieved. Yet they are successful in their rehabilitation, because they can live without being able to walk again, and integrate back into both professional and family life. However, it is very difficult to live life appropriately if there has been a marked change in their thinking and personality.

'With spinal injury, young people would have a sense of a particular outcome, a wheelchair, but with brain injury, we are not just talking about a wheelchair, we are talking about a person never being the same person ever again,' explains Dr Delargy.

He has just come from a meeting with the family of a promising young solicitor who acquired a brain injury after a road crash. She is engaged to be married. Her fiancé and family are expecting more from her than she will ever be able to give. They are hoping the woman they knew will come back to them, will once again drive her car, argue in court, walk up the aisle in her ivory dress. She won't, but her family feel they have reason to hope.

Following the crash, they were told she might not make it through the night. She did. They were then warned that the first week would be touch-and-go. She survived. After a fortnight, doctors said she might never wake up from her coma, and if she did, she might not be able to communicate. She woke up and talked again. Now, two months later, the family has been informed that the chances of her returning to normal mobility and a normal life are very poor.

'There is an inherent difficulty in giving people information which is highly unpalatable for them. Within this woman's family, there is a sense of disbelief. She doesn't look severely injured, the external marks of the crash were limited; there is a sense of progress every time they visit, but what they need to realise is the rate of that progress. In terms of a marathon race, she is going to take all day to finish the marathon. She is not going to finish the marathon in any reasonable time.'

The young solicitor is not fully aware of the changes in her personality. She does not know that she has become more difficult company, that she now says things that would be better left unsaid. 'Those with changed personalities don't necessarily suffer as much as the people around them, who want them to be as they were. In some ways, the brain-injured person is more easily able to accept how they are. Sometimes they can't remember the previous personality and can get annoyed with people who want them to be as they were. The trouble with brain injury recovery is that while you can recover to some extent for many years, the quality and extent of your recovery is best in the immediate aftermath of the crash. The more recovery you make in week one or week two, the more likely you are to get closer to the target of full recovery. After three to six months, it is very difficult to see the person return to a lifestyle or path that they were pursuing,' says Dr Delargy.

He meets spouses who have become carers and young couples who are about to be married. What happens to their plan? How does he advise them? He says that he would always urge them to be patient, to put any plans on hold. 'You have not actually signed up to "for better or for worse". This is the "for worse" bit before you tie the knot. Your partner is never going to be able to be a parent in the normal sense. If somebody is months away from their wedding, our counsel would be to wait, for God's sake, wait. Some people go ahead. Maybe they think that it is curative, but this situation, this condition, is not recoverable. A brain injury is for life.'

Once discharged from the hospital, brain injury patients can find life extremely challenging and, in many cases, lonely. They may have to change their peer group. 'In general, even though you are back on your feet and can talk, you will fall behind your peers. Young men might have no job, relationship, car, house, or career prospects. There is a crippling sense of being left behind. The world was probably something exciting. Now you have little money, you may want to go out, when other people are getting tied down by family and work responsibilities, whereas you might have loads of time on your hands. That sense of isolation is a real core problem within the brain injury group.'

To help combat this problem, the hospital offers a residential rehabilitative training programme for patients with brain injuries. It acts as a halfway house for patients and aims to improve their quality of life by enhancing their social skills. Up to twenty trainees participate in the course; most are young men who have been injured in road collisions.

A dark-haired man in his mid-twenties is making coffee in the kitchen. Hand-painted pictures decorate the magnolia walls and a moulded sculpture of James Joyce's face sits on the shelf. 'We celebrated Bloomsday here, and made his face,' the man explains. He is a long-term resident of the centre. A native of Kerry, he was involved in a car crash near Perth in Western Australia. He woke up in a hospital bed. It was only when he received a pay cheque from the same hospital that he realised it was also where he had begun working as a porter just days before the crash. His memory of everything in the weeks before the crash had been obliterated. He had been enjoying a year out in Australia, living for the moment, embracing an exciting new lifestyle in the sun. Today he is making coffee on his own, a further step towards independent living.

Occupational therapist Anne-Marie McDonald, who works in the unit, says, 'All the trainees do individual and group therapy work. They get counselling and computer training.' She points out a young man who is learning the basics in information technology: how to switch on a computer and create a document. He used to be an accountant for Ericsson.

Back in the occupational therapy unit in the main hospital, patients are participating in the afternoon session. A middle-aged woman wearing a head brace is playing the popular children's game Connect Four in an effort to improve her coordination skills. Another patient is sorting out coloured blocks, as if nothing else in the world mattered. In the corner is a makeshift car, where a young man in a wheelchair is being shown how to transfer himself from his chair into the car seat. He shouts out in frustration. The activity is taking all his strength. His will is weak. Being paralysed can do that.

Adapting to life as a paraplegic takes time; it is a long and arduous journey towards acceptance. Mark Rohan, a former County footballer with Westmeath, knows just how hard it can be. The apprentice electrician was just twenty years old when he crashed his motorbike near his home in Athlone on 4 November 2001. The smash left him paralysed. He spent six months in the National Rehabilitation Hospital, which he still visits for annual check-ups.

It was 9.30 a.m. on a Sunday morning. Driving conditions were good; the road was dry. He had been due to play a match in Athlone, but it was cancelled. Sports-mad Mark also played soccer. He knew his soccer team had a match in Tullamore, County Offaly, and he called to say that he would be able to play after all. He was driving up a steep incline when the bike went out of control, flinging him into the ditch. He smashed head first into a tree, breaking four bones in his back. The road was clear, no other vehicles were involved. Nobody saw the crash happen, and nobody knew that he was lying in the ditch. The bike was thrown on the side of the road, abandoned. For forty minutes, Mark lay on the cold ground, waiting. Shivering, and unable to move, he knew that he had crashed. For some reason, he thought he was under a railway bridge. He could hear trains coming along the tracks, as he fell in and out of consciousness.

A health and safety worker was on his way to Mass when he noticed a motorbike dumped by the roadside. He was about to drive on, but instinct told him to take a closer look. Stopping the car, he thought that the bike had simply been discarded. There was no sign of life anywhere; no helmets or gloves strewn across the tarmac. He decided to check the ditch just in case, a decision that probably saved Mark's life. On discovering Mark, he talked to him, asking him for his name and where he was from. He called for an ambulance, and Mark was taken to Tullamore General Hospital.

En route, Mark's mobile phone was constantly ringing. It was his soccer teammates, wondering why he had not turned up for the match. Later that day, they visited him in the hospital ward. Mark does not remember much about the day, except that he felt extremely cold. He also found it difficult to breathe owing to his broken ribs. He suffered some internal bleeding and was transferred to the Mater Hospital in Dublin. Mark had a compound fracture in his foot, but he still had no idea that he would never walk again.

While in the spinal injuries unit of the Mater Hosptial, Mark was put into a striker bed, an experience he will never forget. The revolving bed system, designed to prevent bed sores, is used for most spinal injury patients when they are first admitted to hospital. 'I felt like a pig being roasted on a spit. I was on my back for four hours; then turned over on my front for four hours. I was staring at the ceiling or the floor. Visitors had to crawl under the bed to talk to me. It was during a four-hour stint when I was facing the floor that I began to realise that something serious was wrong.'

Later, he asked the doctor about the compound fracture on his foot. 'When will you be operating to fix the bone?' Mark said. He needed to know for football. He could then calculate how long it would take him to get back training. 'The doctor told me he was not going to operate on my foot because there would be no point,' Mark recalls. That was all the confirmation he needed. He would never play football for his county again. In fact, he would never walk again.

'The doctors spent a lot of time talking. They told me that my hands were okay, that I could lead a normal life. I was in the striker bed for about two weeks before being put in a body cast for a further twelve weeks. After two weeks in the Mater, I was moved to the National Rehabilitation Hospital.'

From the time he was admitted, Mark was focused on gaining strength and independence. He wanted to be in a position to leave Rehab as quickly as possible. There were times when he broke down. He remembers one late night in the spinal injuries intensive care unit: his family had gone home. The ward was sleeping, the lighting low. He opened his eyes, willing himself to feel his legs again, but they were dead to him. Thinking about the hopelessness of his situation, Mark began to cry. Once he started, he couldn't stop. A nurse came over to comfort him. He told her that the thing that frightened him the most was the fear of the unknown. 'I don't know what is going to happen to me from here on,' he confided.

Nine years down the road, Mark is an All-Ireland Sporting Champion. He captained the national Wheelchair Basketball Team, bringing them to the European Championships on three occasions. He is also a reigning champion in the Irish Open Wheelchair Tennis. Having just completed a degree in Sports Management in University College Dublin, Mark believes that his love of sport helped him to overcome his injury.

But before these remarkable sporting achievements, this courageous young man had to learn how to go to the bathroom and dress himself again. 'It is so hard having people do things for you. It is embarrassing. I had to learn to put on my socks. I remember the first day I sat up. It was a month and a half after the accident, and such a big deal. When you are lying in bed, the one thing you look forward to is getting into a chair. That is the way you are driven in the National Rehabilitation Hospital – small goals.'

When he was first transferred to a wheelchair, Mark refused to let anybody push him. 'I said: if I'm going to get into this chair, I'm going to push myself.' While in the hospital, he took driving lessons, and soon afterwards invested in a disabled driver car.

His girlfriend at the time stood by him through it all, but Mark eventually finished the relationship. 'She always thought that I would walk again. She was convinced. She told me that we would not get married until I was able to walk down the aisle.'

During his stint in Rehab, Mark met patients who were worse off than him. 'I am paralysed from the T3 to T6 sections of the spine. T stands for thoracic injuries. The sections along the spinal cord are divided from T1 to T12. Injuries at or below the thoracic spinal levels result in paraplegia; functions of the hands, arms, neck are not usually affected. There are generally no breathing difficulties. The lower the level of injury, the less severe the effects,' Mark explains. 'You see all sorts in here, patients cursing and throwing things at the staff, others who only have use of their heads. One piece of advice that I took with me was from a patient who had been paralysed for ten years, who was in for an annual check-up: he told me not to be one of those guys who sit around waiting for a cure. Just forget that. Be happy with what you have and get on with it. There may be stem-cell research, but there is no cure for my condition.'

Mark is a firm believer in life after a crash. It may not be the life you envisage, but it is worth living to the full. 'I never thought "why me?" I'm lucky that I became fully independent again. If I wasn't, I would crack up.'

Mark finds going to football matches difficult, watching some players, knowing that he could do better, if only he had the use of his legs again. 'At moments like that, when on the sidelines, I suddenly think, I'm missing out here.' He also finds that people treat him differently, especially women. 'They don't approach me like they used to. They would not know exactly how to behave and would feel sorry for me. They look at me as if to say, "ah the poor creature".'

The patients in the National Rehabilitation Hospital are not to be pitied. They display remarkable courage on a daily basis. All the things we take for granted become vital. They struggle to find the necessary building blocks to get on with their lives, in whatever way they can. They are grateful and, in many cases, lucky to be alive. As Dr Delargy says, 'No matter what you have lost through disability, the majority of people say that it is better than not living.'

The National Rehabilitation Hospital has 119 beds. It is widely accepted that this falls far short of what is needed. Each year about 1,500 people need hospital care for up to one year after brain injuries, according to rehabilitation consultants. Planning permission has been granted for a replacement 230-bed hospital to be built on the site, but promised funding has not been sanctioned, and construction has yet to get under way.

9

ON THE FRONT LINE

'The sights and sounds you see and hear at fatal car crashes stay with you forever.' Garda Declan Egan

When Garda Declan Egan arrives home after a day's work, he sometimes cannot switch off. It is impossible to relax in front of the television if part of your day involves trying to save a child's life on the side of a road. Every trainee garda knows that he or she is likely to encounter traumatic events such as murder scenes and car crashes. It is what they sign up to, but it is only through experience that they learn the full extent of what that means.

Garda Egan was excited to join the Traffic Corps as a motorbike officer in 1999. No two days were the same. He provided escorts, policed bus lanes, and assisted with Operation Freeflow, checked for seat belts, tax, insurance and drink-driving. He refers to these duties as the 'bread and butter' of the Traffic Corps. But there is another side to the job. Spending eight hours on a motorbike in the streets of the capital also involves responding to car crashes. Garda Egan has been to the scene of seven fatal road crashes. He knows the names of everyone who was killed in the collisions; he remembers their faces. He cannot forget those individuals who died in front of him.

'The sights and sounds you see and hear at fatal car crashes stay with you forever. They never go away, what people are wearing, the names of the families. You are dealing with them for weeks and months afterwards. You develop a relationship with people – links that go beyond work,' he says.

Garda Egan has tried to save lives. He attempted to revive a nine-year-old girl while her parents were trapped in their car. What he did in those few minutes meant everything to that family. He recalls vividly the morning he came across the crash. The morning shift had been quiet; he was on patrol in the north Dublin area. There had been no major incidents or traffic problems to report. That was about to change. While driving along a country road on the outskirts of the city, he heard a thundering sound as he approached a bad bend. He turned the corner to find that a car had veered off the road and crashed into a pole. A stream of black smoke was rising from the vehicle. Garda Egan was the first on the scene and immediately radioed for an ambulance. He sprinted towards the car, which was embedded in the ditch. Two people were slumped over what was left of the dashboard. Most of the front of the car had been obliterated. Both front-seat passengers had been wearing seat belts, but the car had not carried airbags.

'I thought they were dead. I wanted to be anywhere else in the world. But I was there. I was working and I had to try to help these people, because they were someone's mum or dad,' he says. He started to shout at the couple through the closed window and was relieved to see some reaction from the male driver. Shortly afterwards, the woman in the passenger seat also started to move slightly. 'They were husband and wife, both trapped and very badly injured. They started to scream, demanding to know what had happened and where they were. I told them not to worry, that they were alive and an ambulance was on its way.'

Garda Egan felt a further wave of relief wash over him. This was not as bad as he had first anticipated. Both individuals were conscious and speaking. He hoped they would pull through and recover in time. For now, he would stay with them, keep them talking and offer as much encouragement as he could. He turned towards the road briefly, straining his ears for the sound of the ambulance siren. Instead, he heard a screeching sound coming from the woman in passenger seat. She was shouting hysterically. 'Mary, Mary! Where is Mary?'

Garda Egan tried to calm her down.

'Who is Mary?'

'Mary is our daughter.'

'Don't worry about Mary. Whoever is minding her will be looking after her fine. Try to focus on yourselves.' The driver of the car then told him that Mary had been in the back seat. The family were on their way to a party. The back seat was empty, except for a pink rucksack. Garda Egan assumed that they had already dropped off their daughter. They must be confused or in shock after the impact, he thought. The couple, now crying out in desperation, remained insistent that Mary had been with them when they crashed.

Garda Egan scanned the area, a single carriageway country road with overgrown ditches on either side. In the distance, about 40 metres in front of the car, something caught his eye. It was a pink and white plastic item, lying on top of some bushes. He discovered it was a child's shoe, a runner with the laces still tied. He felt a knot in his stomach. The smell of burning rubber was strong. He was about to come across an image that he will never be able to forget. Mary, whom he learned later was nine, was lying in the ditch, among the brambles and barbed wire; most of her clothes – a tank top, mini-skirt and jeans – had been torn. Her skin had been scraped along the tarmac.

'I pulled her out as best I could and I administered CPR,' says Garda Egan. 'Her face was so badly damaged that it took me a few seconds to find her mouth. I gave her mouth-to-mouth for six minutes until the ambulance crew arrived. I remember them pulling me away, but you don't stop; they literally had to drag me away from her. She was dead and there was nothing I could do, but you have this notion – you see it in the movies when people come back to life. There were holes in her neck and chest. I could feel my own breath coming back at me, and she died. She was dead when I got there and there was nothing I could do to bring her back.'

Days later, when Mary was being laid to rest, the family asked Garda Egan to help carry her white coffin. He obliged. 'At first I thought, why me? What did I do? I'm sure they had other family and friends. I suppose what I forgot was that while they were stuck in their car, completely helpless, they were looking at me for six minutes on my knees trying to bring their daughter back to life.'

For Garda Egan, having to carry that small, white coffin was difficult. He admits that it was almost as hard as the day of the crash. 'People don't think about the ripple effect of car crashes. They focus on the families, and of course they should. But the Guards can also be affected. I had to deal with this lifeless little girl lying on the road as work. I had to not think about her parents, who were looking at me and how dreadful it must have been for them. I had to focus on the job; these were people in need and what could I do to make their situation better? A day like that is not easy to get past.'

Garda Egan was unable to drive himself home from work after his shift. A colleague brought him to his door. Sleeping was not an option. 'I didn't sleep for days. I was thinking could I have done something differently. In that situation, I couldn't, but I wanted to be the superman, the hero. I wanted to save the day, make things better, fix it. That is what everyone wants – the ambulance crew after me, the doctors in the hospital. But sometimes it is simply not achievable,' he says. 'I have kids myself. If I had no children, it would not make it any easier. None of us are designed to see a nine-year-old child ending up like that . . . You cope by talking about it, and that can be enough.'

Professional counselling services are made available to the gardaí. There is a peer support system within the force. When members are exposed to traumatic events like fatal car crashes, they are encouraged to talk through any issues with their colleagues or with professionals. If post-traumatic stress syndrome strikes, then professional medical care is offered to deal with the problem. 'Sometimes it's enough to talk to a close friend, colleague or loved one. The important thing is to get it out of your system,' says Garda Egan.

Garda Declan Egan now talks about his experiences for a living. He has moved to the Road Safety Unit of the Garda Traffic Corps. The Dublin-based road safety department, which comprises a sergeant and two gardaí, was established in 2004. The role of the team is to promote road safety to schools and businesses. This is done through a hard-hitting presentation called 'It won't happen to me'.

'We can talk about the reality of road carnage, the things you don't see on the news: the bodies in cars, the knocking on doors at 2 a.m. to deliver the bad news. We give an audience a sense that people die. We try to personalise it, bring in the fact that this could be your brother, sister, mother or father. We aim to instil a sense of loss; extract some kind of sympathy from an audience. No one ever thinks it is going to happen to them, to their family, but it might. You could be on the news tonight for all the wrong reasons.'

Garda Egan also worked as a family liaison officer. He was specifically trained to deal with families in the aftermath of fatal car crashes. 'Everything becomes so important because people remember everything. That is why it is so important for us to get it right, because families remember exactly what the Guard said, how he said it, the degree of sympathy he showed at the scene. We need to be really alert and know what to do in these situations. There are certain unpleasant things that we need to discuss with people when gathering the facts. Awkward questions may need to be asked and funeral arrangements may need to be organised. People don't focus on the aftermath, when the crash has happened and the funeral is over. We ask an audience to consider what happens next. What about the personal belongings of the victim? Who goes through the private things that made that person unique, the box under the bed with prized letters or photos, the saved articles or trinkets? Where does it go?' says Garda Egan. 'Nine out of ten people who are killed on our roads make the wrong choices, driving while tired, not wearing a seat belt, speeding, drink-driving, overtaking in the wrong place, not paying attention. Our job is to encourage people to make the right decisions. We can't be in the car with you, but we can educate. Our ultimate goal is to change driver behaviour.'

The Garda Road Safety Unit continues to develop the 'It won't happen to me' programme, and has trained up to 100 gardaí nationwide in an effort to bring it to more schools and businesses.

Emergency Services

'Telling somebody that, despite my best efforts, their child is dead is the most difficult part of my job.' Dr Gerry Lane

Emergency consultant Dr Gerry Lane has a formula. When he trained as a senior registrar, the doctor, who works in Letterkenny General Hospital in County Donegal, learned how best to tell parents that their child was dead. The key to this difficult task was repetition.

'You have to make sure they get the message, so you tend to say he/she is dead at least four different times in four different ways in the first couple of minutes. Telling somebody that, despite my best efforts, their child is dead is the most difficult part of my job. I try to be as sensitive as possible, give them a few moments to take it in, but I then have to repeat the fact, and I feel terrible. You know that scene in the movie *Psycho*, where Perkins stabs the victim four times – that is what I feel like. "He's dead, I'm very sorry, he's dead, I've told the coroner that he's dead, I'm sorry he's dead." There is no mercy. There is no hiding. There is no escape. I go into a small, horrible room with these people and they see it coming. They know it is coming and then they get it, bang, bang, bang, bang, and their illusions are destroyed.'

Dr Lane first joined the staff at Letterkenny General Hospital in July 2001 but admits that his job gets no easier with the passage of time. Every year he deals with more than 1,000 patients who are seriously injured in road crashes in Donegal – that equates to three people every day. 'It is wearing and frustrating. Road deaths are just the tip of the iceberg. They are the headline grabber, but behind every dead person, there are up to ten injured people, who are admitted to hospital as a direct result of car crashes. They are taking up beds. The average age of those patients in my hospital is eighteen.'

Dr Lane says that his medical teams deal with major trauma on a regular basis, 'We are so used to major trauma from car crashes that it is almost a knee-jerk reaction for us.' He commends the system that is in place. It begins with the ambulance personnel, who inform the emergency department to be on standby for a major incident. Like emergency departments across the country, the one in Letterkenny is usually packed with patients. If the hospital has been alerted about a major incident, then the waiting room has to be emptied within fifteen minutes. 'Our place is always busy. If we have a big smash coming in, we send the walking wounded home. We get beds available. Some patients have to double up. I orchestrate what needs to be done, assign the team members their various roles,' Dr Lane explains.

The sound of sirens also indicates to Dr Lane that he is about to have a busy day. 'Sirens have different frequencies – ambulances, patrol cars, fire engines. When you hear more than one, you know it's going to be big.' As the team leader, Dr Lane also has to remove any distractions. Medical teams can be stopped in their tracks at the sight of a dead child. 'Dead people are a very bad distraction. If you have a dead child in an emergency department, suddenly you don't have twenty professionals, you have twenty human beings.'

Dr Lane recalls one example of when paramedics rushed a five-month-old baby boy into Emergency. He was one of a number of victims involved in a bad car crash. A group of nurses and doctors gathered around the child. They forgot about their individual roles and focused on the helpless child. The paramedic had already performed CPR on the baby, but sadly he never regained consciousness. Dr Lane approached the circle. 'The child is dead,' he said. No one moved. He approached the paramedic with a blanket and gently took the baby from his arms. 'I wrapped him up in a blanket and I swaddled him like the baby Jesus, his little face showing. I put the baby in a little cot in a quiet room and asked a student nurse to watch the door,' he says.

'An ambulance driver will always pull out a kid. A driver will always think a child may have a chance. Everyone does their best to save lives.' Sometimes patients are so seriously injured, they may need to be transferred to Beaumont Hospital in Dublin. Dr Lane ensures that patients are moved in a safe and fast way.

Coming face to face with the devastating consequences of road crashes on a regular basis has influenced the way Dr Lane thinks about road carnage. He has strong views on the subject, believing that many of the crashes he has seen were preventable. 'My personal belief is that most road collisions are as preventable as the measles. If everybody got the MMR vaccination, then we wouldn't have the measles. If I could invent a pill or a shot and could give it to 4.4 million people in this country, I could cut down the number of road deaths and be the most famous doctor in the world. This shot would have four ingredients: cop on, slow down, belt up and back off. An accident has got a judgment built into it, that this is an act of God, not preventable, not predictable, like being hit by lightning. That's not true for road collisions, because most of them are predictable and many are preventable. Road deaths are very often due to ordinary people with ordinary lives making bad decisions. We need to ask for small changes from a large number of people.'

Dr Lane believes that drugs are a factor when it comes to road collisions. 'Drugs are a major concern. We don't test for them routinely. It is an emerging problem. Data suggests that a large number of people who tested negative for alcohol, would, if tested, test positive for drugs. There are other forms of impairment, the result of tiredness or exhaustion.'

Dr Lane's steadfast view on drink-driving is that there is no safe level of alcohol in the blood. 'Even if the concentration of alcohol is just 50 mg of alcohol per 100 ml of blood, you are four times more likely to have a collision than if you have none. There is no safe amount. There is nothing I can do to stop from being horrified. I can't stop being aghast at the waste of life, the carnage, the slaughter. It is slaughter. At times I think the last car crash was the most horrific, but the depressing thing is I never have to wait very long for another one that is just as bad.'

Dr Gerry Lane highlights the importance of wearing seat belts. He knows what not wearing a seat belt – or even wearing it the wrong way – can mean. 'Brain damage or spinal injury is not just for the weekend. It's for life,' he says. 'Imagine being thirty years of age and having to get your mother to look after the manual evacuation of your bowels. I know of young men in the most rural parts of Donegal who have been left paralysed. Their parents have had to take out costly loans to renovate the house, making it wheelchair-friendly. Their significant other is no longer interested in a relationship. What is going to happen to those young men in twenty years time, when their elderly parents are no longer able to lift them? The next step for them is to go into care. Imagine always having to depend on carers.

'When you go into a room and tell parents that their son is alive, but has a spinal injury, they are, at first, overjoyed that their child has survived. There is hope, happiness, smiles, just like on TV, but then the little candle in their eyes dampens down and I know that they are not fully hearing or understanding what I'm saying. You might survive a crash, but your life, as you knew it, is effectively over.'

Fire Service

'There is no kind of training that can prepare you for comng across such scenes of carnage.' Michael Comer

Michael Comer has worked with the fire service for forty-two years. He has never got used to seeing dead bodies. The fire-officer from Swinford, County Mayo, was just seventeen years old when he attended his first fatal road traffic crash. It happened close to his home where a tractor had overturned on a bend. A boy was trapped under the Massey Ferguson. Michael helped to extricate the boy's body. The sixteen-year-old local lad was dead. He had been a neighbour – a young man he had known all his life. Michael remembers lifting his body from the ditch on to an embankment by the side of the road. It was winter; the frost-tipped grass felt rough. 'The wheel nut of the tractor had come loose and lodged under his eye. I can still see that clearly, how his face had transformed. It was horrible,' Michael recalls.

The graphic nature of the crash did not deter Michael from the job in hand. At no stage did he question the sometimes gruesome reality of what he had signed up to. It was a job, he was there to help and he was happy to be able to offer some assistance. This prevailing attitude stayed with him for the next four decades.

'It is traumatic, but that is part of this job. You get paid to do this. You have to be professional. You can't go to pieces because that won't help anybody. You park your emotions and you deal with the tasks. You can get emotional afterwards if you want to,' he explains. 'Every injury or death on the roads is equally traumatic. I have seen a lot of multiple fatalities in forty-two years, and they are all deeply troubling incidents. There is no kind of training that can prepare you for coming across such scenes of carnage. How do you deal with it? You talk about it.'

Michael has been attached to the Swinford Fire Brigade all his life. His colleagues have become his best friends. Their shared experiences have brought them closer together. After a particularly traumatic car crash, they might retire to the station to talk about what they have just witnessed, and assess how they worked as a team. Sometimes they go for a drink together. This helps the group get past the initial shock of such call-outs. At their weekly fire meetings, they once again go through in a professional manner the steps they took, how they performed, and how a particular crash impacted on them.

Michael points out that there is professional counselling available, provided for by Mayo County Council, but, he says, if desired, it must be requested by an officer. In 1967 when he first joined up, there was no such facility. Indeed, he has seen many aspects of the fire service improve over time, including the range of equipment used to cut people from cars.

'In general terms the role of the fire officer at a road traffic crash is rescue; to get injured people out who are trapped in cars. We have the tools and the training to get people out. In the late 1960s and early 1970s, the tools used to be so basic. It was a hammer, a chisel and a steel lever – that was the extent of our cutting equipment and the cars were made of heavier steel, making the jobs quite frustrating. Nowadays, we have the most modern, standardised and up-to-date kit from search-lighting to all sorts of cutting, forcing and pushing equipment. There is really no job beyond us. You could go to any crash with confidence and know you could extricate the person quickly, effectively and efficiently. The apparatus began to improve in the 1980s and got progressively better. For the last fifteen years, it has been superb.'

With the advent of technological advances, Michael and his colleagues have had to attend various training courses. They also take refresher courses every year, which focus on how best to cut people out of the wreckage, how equipment works and how to treat people at the scene. 'The idea is that you cut the car from around the person,' he says. 'You don't move the person as that might cause damage, so you tear or bite or strip the car away from them.'

One officer is usually assigned to stay with the trapped person in the car. 'He tells the person his name, continues to talk, and maintains eye contact. This reassures the person that there is someone with them; that help has arrived. It also helps to keep them focused, to keep them calm.'

'Don't hurt me any more. My arm. My leg. Will I be able to walk again? My baby.' These are the kinds of incessant phrases that Michael has heard from injured people trapped in cars. 'The people who are conscious and in pain are the most distressed. You won't die from broken limbs, but people will scream because of the excruciating pain,' says Michael. There is no rush with a job when an unfortunate person has passed away. If people are alive, speed is the number one priority because there is what is termed a golden hour between the crash happening and the person arriving in hospital. If you get them there within sixty minutes, then the person has a higher percentage chance of survival.'

In the late 1970s, Michael Comer married and became a father. He admits that his reaction to harrowing crashes changed once he became a family man. Coming face to face with road carnage was more distressing, disturbing and upsetting, especially when he found himself thinking about his young wife and daughters at home. He recalls an incident that shook him.

It was late one summer night when his beeper sounded. The roads were wet. Michael arrived on the scene of the crash: an upturned car by the side of the road. A young married couple had been driving home after a night out. They were parents to two little girls. The fire crew managed to extricate the driver from the car. He was dazed, disorientated and in a state of shock. Michael believes there was also a distinct smell of alcohol from the man. He sat on the embankment, waiting for his wife to be rescued. But his wife was dead, her neck broken. She was trapped in an awkward position between the front window of the car and the ditch. It took some time before the fire officers could move the car in order to lift the body from the wreckage. 'We got the lads to lift the back of the car. One of the officers climbed in to reach her head and I managed to grab hold of her legs. We lifted her as gently as we could from the car. I will never forget it. I even remember the colour of her tights. We covered her in a sheet and laid her onto a straight board. The driver was unaware that his wife was dead. He was still sitting down, asking us was she okay.'

That evening, as Michael made the journey back to his family bungalow overlooking the town of Swinford, he could not get the image of the dead woman out of his head. He thought about the two children she had left behind, who were still fast asleep, who had no idea that they would wake up motherless. Those two little girls were the same ages as his own daughters and the dead woman was twenty-seven, the same age as his wife. 'I have flashbacks of road traffic crashes, especially that one, even now, thirty years later,' he says.

Michael believes that road safety has improved beyond all recognition. As a young fire officer in the 1970s, he found it scandalous that there were up to two deaths a day on Irish roads and little mention of the startling fact on the national airwaves, press or in schools. 'I couldn't believe the number of bad crashes that I was being called out to, and the fact that nobody talked about it. People just shrugged it off and accepted it as part of modern living.'

In recent years, when the opportunity to get involved with promoting road safety came his way, Michael signed up without hesitation. He was contacted by Noel Gibbons, the Road Safety Officer for County Mayo, who asked him to take part in a hard-hitting educational roadshow for secondary schools across the region. The initiative was a complete success, gaining nationwide recognition and being copied by a number of other local authorities in Ireland. 'The roadshow works,' Michael says, 'because it comes down to the students' level.'

Picture the scene. Up to nine hundred students arrive at the event. Class is cancelled for the afternoon; the mood is jubilant, upbeat. Throngs of excited girls giggle, chew gum and gossip about the latest celebrity news or the new boy in school. The lads are stopped in their tracks by the Ferrari parked by the front door of the large gym. It has been polished to perfection. They imagine James Bond, beautiful girls and speeding on an open road through the desert somewhere in Arizona. Ogling the red motor, they move closer to take in the leather-seated slick interior, and form a haphazard queue to get a chance to sit in the driver seat. It's not quite a test drive, but the students at least get a feel for the sports car.

On arrival in the sports hall, the disc jockey on the stage is pumping out the latest chart-topping tunes. Flashing strobe lighting brightens the room. Students display their hip-hop moves, while others just clap and sing along to the chorus. Friends play requests for each other, enjoying the party atmosphere. 'It is a feel-good day,' says Michael, 'then you hit them with this smack in the mouth that is so extreme many of them get sick, vomit under their seats.'

A young male driver is the first person on stage. He wheels himself up the side ramp and tells the story of how he ended up in a wheelchair. Sean had been speeding. He misjudged the space between him and an oncoming car as he moved to overtake. The former football fanatic will never walk again. As his speech comes to a close, a large photo of him is suspended from the stage. In it, he is able-bodied, holding a bright gold trophy with the inscription 'Man of the Match'.

The presentation continues with a strong and powerful graphic slideshow outlining exactly what can happen in a road traffic crash, just how devastating it can be. The film focuses on a young man who goes out for the evening with his friends and never comes home. He is the same age as the students in the audience. He is killed when the car in which he is a passenger smashes into a wall at speed.

Members of the emergency services then take to the stage to explain their various roles when called to the scene of a bad crash. 'We tell it like it is,' says Michael, 'all the gory details. The music, laughing and joking quickly disappear. They see the damage that can result from a car crash and they meet a real-life person, a young man, a few years older than them, and they suddenly stop and think.' The presentation ends with a parent, who speaks to the students about the unbearable loss of her son who was killed in a road traffic crash. 'This type of roadshow impacts on these kids. It makes them see that it could happen to them. They get shown how they can make sure it doesn't happen to them. I'm sure the impact may fade over time, but I also think it is installed so shockingly that it has a long-term effect. The presentation shocks, because all of it is true.'

Michael has never become immune or desensitised to the devastating scenarios he has encountered because of his job. 'I have had to pick up body parts from the side of the road and put them together like a jigsaw puzzle. I have had to search for the charred remains of children in the rubble of a burnt-out car. I have seen people badly burned, people with so many broken bones, frightened people hanging on to this life by a thread.' He recalls an incident near Knock Airport in 1988. A truck driver lost control of the vehicle at speed. It overturned. A cold-freeze container at the back of the lorry was full of meat joints which scattered across the scene. 'There was about 28 tonnes of meat in a fridge; bits of beef were all over the road. We had to find parts of the driver's body in amongst the meat. We were there for the best part of four hours searching slowly for all of his remains. It was one of the worst scenes I ever came across in my forty-two years' service.'

Michael Comer retired from the fire service in June 2009. He reiterates that the trick to his job was to always adopt a professional approach. 'It is not you who is in trouble; they are. You are there to help, that is your function. You are there to help render assistance and put order on a chaotic situation. And you get a lot of situations when you can help, when you can render the kind of assistance that makes it all worthwhile, when you can help save a life.'

Ambulance Service

'Taking a road crash victim out of a car can be very difficult because the body, though lifeless, can still be very warm.' Keith Mullane, Advanced Paramedic

'The injuries are incompatible with life.' When a doctor is called to the scene of a crash or to a hospital morgue to pronounce someone dead, that is how he says it; the terminology used when a neck has snapped or a heart has stopped owing to a traumatic situation. It is a phrase that advanced paramedic Keith Mullane both dreads, and expects, during his work with the Limerick Ambulance Service. Over the past ten years, he has experienced a series of what are termed 'bad calls', when his unit has responded to a number of horrific car crashes in a relatively short space of time.

He says that at first details are usually sketchy. 'Several calls may come in for the same crash, with a lot of panic and emotional upset on the line.' Once dispatched, Keith never knows exactly what to expect. Instead of pre-empting the scene, he concentrates instead on the type of equipment on board, preparing himself mentally for the impending task. 'A classic car crash involves two cars on a country road,' he says. 'On arrival at the scene, the first thing I'm met with is debris: bits of broken cars, bumpers, skid marks, glass. There could be people trapped in one car while others walk around the road, dazed, confused and bloody. People are screaming for help. I notice personal belongings on the road, things like local GAA gear bags or Brown Thomas shopping bags.'

Keith welcomes the screams. It means the occupants of the cars are alive. He goes through a series of checks for any significant blood loss or possible spinal injuries. 'I may not want to move someone, but I also have to think that this car could be unstable, or could catch fire. The difficulty comes when there is someone trapped in a car and needs to get out fast.' Keith explains that the time frame can be crucial. 'A person's condition could rapidly deteriorate. My colleagues and I are often trying to work against the clock. We put a neck brace on, remove the injured person from the car, on to a spinal board, and into the ambulance and continue our management until we hand them over to the local emergency department.'

Keith is trained to save lives. When he arrives too late to do this job, he treats the victims who have already passed away with the utmost dignity and respect. After going through the various medical checks, Keith shuts their eyes. 'I have seen drivers sitting behind the steering wheel with tiny cuts on their foreheads and no other apparent injuries. Their eyes are open, staring into space, always with this look of disbelief, their last thoughts before the crash written all over their unresponsive faces. It is quite surreal.'

It is also strange to hear a discarded mobile phone ring, says Keith. 'If we are removing the body of someone who should have been home fifteen minutes earlier, sometimes we hear their mobile phone. The ring tone persists, from the floor or a handbag. The screen reads "Mum calling" or "Dad calling". I've also seen "My special guy" or "My number one girl". Those people calling have no idea that the person they are looking for will never answer them again. We usually hand the phones over to the gardaí. Taking a road crash victim out of a car can be very difficult because the body, though lifeless, can still be very warm.' He explains that the body is usually placed in a body bag and brought directly to the nearest hospital mortuary. Certain procedures are then followed by the ambulance and hospital staff. 'A doctor confirms our findings. If there is a priest in the hospital, he is sent for, to administer the last rites. The mortuary is a refrigerated area where the body is preserved until a post mortem can be carried out. The body is removed from our stretcher and placed on a stainless steel tray. It is then tagged on the hands and feet. The mortuary logbook is filled out with the personal details of the victim. We place the body into a refrigerated unit, write the name on a whiteboard above it, and close the doors on someone's life. The end of a life is the start of another's grief. That is how we look at it. There is something very unnatural about placing a young person into a refrigerator unit who up until an hour earlier was going about his or her daily life.'

Keith remembers the first time he was called to a serious crash. A young man had been wearing his seatbelt incorrectly, going under his hand rather than across his chest. On impact, the belt somehow managed to break his neck. 'I was only starting out at the time, and I wanted to save him, to resuscitate him, but I knew it was too late.' There have been other occasions where unrestrained people were thrown from cars on impact. 'Some people are unrecognisable due to their horrific injuries.'

The paramedic's job gets even more complicated when relatives arrive on the scene, demanding to see their loved ones. 'The irony is most car crashes happen just a few miles from home. Parents can even get to the scene before we do. It is extremely difficult to tell them that they can't see their child, as they are too severely injured and disfigured. I have had to hold mothers and fathers back from maimed victims. I have seen family members fainting and collapsing on the side of the road. Relatives have suffered chest pain and heart attacks due to the grief and shock. I have had to call a third ambulance to deal with people who were not even involved in a crash, but simply could not cope with what they had witnessed.'

Many car crashes involve a number of family members or friends in the same vehicle. 'I have come across crash scenes with two dead and two very seriously injured people. I have had to literally crawl across the body of someone to get to the person that is alive. I have to do this while constantly trying to bear in mind the dignity of everyone involved. Sometimes, it's just not possible.'

Keith rejects the title 'hero'. 'We are not heroes; we are doing a job that we are trained to do. People have tried to give us money, but we don't accept it. We ask that they donate it instead to charity. We are not looking for a pat on the back – this is what we signed up to do. If we get a run of bad calls, people may need to take time out from the job. The HSE provides counselling known as "Critical incident stress debriefing". Sometimes the best therapy is to speak with a more experienced colleague about your feelings. It does not mean you can't cope. It's better to talk things through; try to avoid taking "baggage" home with you.'

Keith feels privileged to be in his position. 'The traumatic stuff comes, but not as frequently as people think it does. My job makes me appreciate all the good things in my own life so much more. If being a paramedic was that traumatic all the time, we would not be wearing white shirts to work.'

Injured in the Line of Duty

'It was September 11th, my September 11th – the day when everything in my life changed.' Garda Colm Cullen

Garda Colm Cullen has thirty-eight years of service, more than half of which he has spent in a wheelchair. He is attached to the Traffic Division in Dublin Castle. He was on duty as a Garda motorcyclist when a car crashed into him, breaking three bones in his back in 1992. 'It was September 11th, my September 11th,' he recalls, 'the day when everything in my life changed.' The garda, from Naas in County Kildare, was just thirty-eight years of age and the father of two young boys at the time of the crash. Based at Dublin Castle, Garda Cullen could be sent all over the country for the purpose of work. As a member of the motorcycle unit, he often had to help with the traffic policing of big events. On this particular occasion, he was en route to a European cycling event in Cork which was to kick off the following day. He never made it there.

At about 2 p.m., Garda Cullen stopped off at Portlaoise Garda Station to pick up a colleague who was due to work with him in Cork. It turned out his friend was on shift until 4 p.m. that afternoon. Rather than continue on without him, Garda Cullen decided to wait for his colleague. 'We can travel down together on the bikes rather than you go on your own,' he told him, 'I'll hang on here and have a cup of tea while I'm waiting for you.' Later that day, the two drivers set out towards Cork. It was a bright, clear and dry day. Just outside Roscrea, County Tipperary, on a long stretch of straight road, Garda Cullen noticed a parked car on the hard shoulder. The two gardaí cruised along until their bikes were alongside the car. Just at that moment, the driver of the car did a sudden U-turn, pulling out in front of them. 'We were driving parallel to each other and the car. My colleague was on the inside, I was on the outside. He went left and got behind the car, and I went right. I blasted the horn thinking they'll hear the noise, get a fright and jam on the brakes, and stop. I thought I would be all right.' The car smashed into Garda Colm Cullen. He was thrown off the bike, landing the wrong way in the ditch. 'I broke three bones in my back, crushed three vertebrae. I landed on my shoulder, but because the ditch was so soft, my shoulder dug in and my back arched, shattering the vertebrae,' he explains. 'When you are a biker, you expect little tips. I was out and about in Dublin city most days. You expect a scrape or two. The most I ever did was skimmed my knee prior to that.'

While lying on the ground, Garda Cullen knew to start wiggling what he could. He could feel his shoulders working, his hands and arms. His colleague sprinted over. 'How are my legs looking,' Garda Cullen asked, 'because I can't feel them? Are they smashed?' His friend told him they were fine. Garda Cullen knew immediately that he had a problem. The ambulance arrived. He warned the paramedics to be careful when moving him. 'I have a spinal injury,' he said. He was rushed to Nenagh General Hospital in County Tipperary, but later moved by Air Corps helicopter to the national Spinal Injuries Unit in the Mater Hospital in Dublin.

There, he had a series of further X-rays and an MRI scan of his back. Garda Cullen was lying in the spinal injury ward when a surgeon approached his cubicle. Dressed in green scrubs, he drew back the curtains and with a look of concern glanced down at Garda Cullen. 'The minute he looked at me I knew it was bad news. He had that look on his face that said he did not want to be telling me what he had to tell me. I asked him was it bad. He told me that it was. I asked him was it a wheelchair. He told me that it was; that my spinal cord was severed.'

Garda Cullen spent the next fortnight in the Mater Hospital. He underwent surgery to bring down the swelling in his back. He was then placed on a striker bed for a week. 'Striker beds could have been invented by the Gestapo,' he says. 'It was pure torture. I felt like I was lying on an ironing board. At the end of it is a contraption that looks like a ship's wheel. Like a sandwich, I was strapped in and turned up and down throughout the day. I spent a week on that thing, the longest week of my life,' he says.

It is a familiar story for most spinal-injury patients. Once their time in the Mater is complete, they are then transferred to the National Rehabilitation Hospital in Dun Laoghaire. Garda Colm Cullen spent four months in Rehab, learning how to dress, wash, shower and use the toilet on his own. 'The staff are brilliant; the work they do is phenomenal,' he says, 'People don't realise what they can achieve.'

Within a year of his crash, Garda Cullen was back at work, an accomplishment he knows would not have been possible without the dedicated and intensive rehabilitative care he received. 'I went through a period where I wished I had died in the crash. That lasted about two weeks. I thought about the choices I had. I could either sink or swim. I had a young family, my wife and two boys just eight and twelve. If I decided to sink, I would be dragging them down with me. I felt I had no choice but to pull myself together because my family had done nothing to deserve this. They didn't understand what was going on, and suffered psychologically. At the time, Rehab was not quite as family-orientated as it is today. There was no counselling or explanations offered to my two young lads. When my eldest came in and saw me sitting beside my bed in a wheelchair, he ran out crying.'

Once discharged from hospital, Garda Cullen was determined to get back to work. 'I got bored sitting at home, watching television until 2 a.m., waking up at lunchtime. I had no structure or purpose to my days,' he recalls.

Garda Cullen commends the Garda Síochána for being 100 per cent behind him in his decision to return to full-time employment. 'They were extremely accommodating in every way. I was living in a house in Naas that backed onto the Garda Station. They offered to transfer me to Naas and to build a gate into the back wall so that I would not even have to go around the block to get to work.'

Although grateful for their kind offer, Garda Cullen's preference was to stay within the Traffic Corps at Dublin Castle, the place where his friends still worked. He became the duty officer, a role that involved looking after the running of the office on a daily basis. 'I do the paperwork for my unit, the phones, radios and work rotas. Sometimes, I work alone as everyone else is out on the road, but I enjoy it. I decide on logistics, the deployment of jeeps and bikes on any given day.' Garda Cullen has never felt any sense of anger towards the Garda Síochána for his predicament, nor does he blame the motorbike. 'It was not the motorbike that did this to me – it was the car that hit me. I don't blame the driver. We have all made mistakes while driving, failing to look when we should have. It was a terrible accident. We were not going fast as we were not in any rush.' He says the support he has been shown by the force has been phenomenal. 'My Superintendent came to see me and put arrangements in place to convert my house into a wheelchair-adaptable home, with a new toilet, shower and ramps.'

Garda Colm Cullen is one of two officers who have been left disabled owing to a motorbike crash. He is the only member of the force in a wheelchair as a result of a crash that happened at work, while on duty. 'My rehabilitation was going back to work,' he says.

10

'DON'T WAKE ME'

'There were five precious children killed in that car and he didn't even get a year for every life.' Rose O'Connor.

It was a typical Saturday night in the seaside town of Buncrana, County Donegal. A cold drizzle hung in the salty air. Waves crashed against the pier wall; the promenade looked deserted. Punters filed into the pubs, taking refuge from the fast-approaching winter weather. It was early October 2005, the summer a distant memory. Girls in mini-skirts and high heels hopped from one foot to the other at the ATM machine. Smokers huddled in doorways along the main street. Take-away restaurants were doing a steady trade, and minibus drivers had already parked up, waiting to transfer the younger generation to the surrounding nightclubs. But first there was a show in town that everyone wanted to see: a hypnotist had come to Buncrana, drawing large crowds to his act at a local hotel.

Twenty-one-year-old Charlene O'Connor attended the performance with her boyfriend, Gavin Duffy. The childhood sweethearts, who were the same age, had been together for five years, and had plans to get married one day. Charlene had reason to celebrate. Having spent the past four years studying for her Accountancy degree at Letterkenny Institute of Technology, she was due to graduate the following Friday.

Gavin Duffy phoned his first cousin Darren Quinn, inviting him to join them for the show. Gavin and Darren were more like brothers. In school, they shared the same classrooms; as young adults identical jobs. They had both completed apprenticeships together, and had recently set up their own plastering business. The cousins worked with another friend, 23-year-old David Steele, who also chose to meet up with the group for the evening.

Rochelle Peoples, David's girlfriend and Charlene's best friend, was curious about the hypnotist. When her friends called her to join them, the 22-year-old trainee hairdresser went along. Following the gig, the five friends were in high spirits. They passed a swarm of young people queuing for the minibuses. Everyone seemed to be going dancing. The Bailey nightclub in Redcastle would be packed and there was bound to be a great atmosphere at the popular venue. The friends then made a last-minute decision to go to the Bailey. The girls, who had not planned to go clubbing, went home to change their clothes. Rochelle put on a sparkly top, touched up her make-up and did a twirl for her parents, who were in the sitting room watching television. 'How do I look?' she asked. Terry and Rosemarie Peoples admired her outfit, delighted to see her so happy. Rochelle told them she would not be late. 'We are just going for a dance. We won't be long. I'm off tomorrow, though, so please don't wake me.' Her parents smiled, reassuring her that they would allow her to sleep in.

The five friends drove to the Bailey nightclub in David Steele's black Peugeot 306. They drank very little that night, just a few beers between them. Their post mortem results would later reveal that none of them was over the legal alcohol limit when they were killed. On the dance floor, Rochelle bumped into her younger brother and only sibling. Sixteen-year-old Matthew Peoples was not supposed to be there; his parents had no idea. Rochelle would not say anything. The two of them were very close and always looked out for each other. Matthew was wearing a shirt Rochelle had chosen for him. 'You'll look old enough to get in with this on you,' she had told him.

Darren Quinn was chatting to his brother Shane, who was also enjoying a night out in the Bailey. The DJ was playing tunes that everybody loved. Dancing the night away, Charlene, Rochelle, Darren, Gavin and David were thrilled to be together. The time seemed to race past, and before long the fluorescent lights signalled the end of the night. Sweaty teenagers darted to the cloakroom. Some couples kissed in corner seats near the bar, oblivious of the harsh light. Throngs of people spilled out into the rain, hailing taxis and dashing towards packed minibuses. As the five friends left, Gavin Duffy, who was insured to drive David Steele's car, volunteered to be the designated driver. He was sober and would get them home safe and sound. Weather conditions were poor; the winding narrow roads of the Inishowen Peninsula were wet, and relatively busy with nightclub traffic. Gavin Duffy was driving responsibly and within the speed limit. He overtook taxi driver Eamon McKinney at about 60 miles per hour on a straight part of the road with a broken white line. Minutes later, Eamon McKinney would see the black Peugeot car again, but it would take him some time to recognise it. After overtaking the taxi, Gavin Duffy continued on in the direction of Buncrana. He was driving within the speed limit on his side of the road. At the same time, 47-year-old Brendan Henderson was driving his blue Mazda people-carrier in the opposite direction. The psychiatric nurse was coming from the Pollan Beach Hotel where he had been drinking alcohol for approximately eight hours. At 3 a.m., he left the hotel drunk, and got behind the wheel of his car. He was speeding; his car was on the wrong side of the road. In the remote townland of Cross, halfway between Carndonagh and Quigley's Point, at a twisting section of the road, Brendan Henderson's Mazda ploughed head-on into the Peugeot, killing all five people inside.

Taxi-driver Eamon McKinney was the first person to come on the scene of the crash. He saw the Peugeot on the grass verge and the Mazda in the middle of the road. His passengers alerted the emergency services. Emma Noone and her friends jumped out of the taxi. They shouted to the people in the black car. Silence. Emma then got sick from shock at the side of the road.

Shane Quinn, who had been talking to his brother Darren ten minutes earlier in the nightclub, was four cars behind the crash. He stopped his car, wondering what the delay was. He ran towards the wreckage. 'When I saw the black car, I just knew it was David Steele's car. I knew it was badly smashed and got the feeling they were all dead. I saw my cousin Gavin. His head was hanging out the driver's door and I knew automatically he was dead,' he says. In shock, Shane called his mother, Pauline Quinn. 'There's been a bad accident,' he told her, 'Darren and Gavin are dead.'

A short time later, a minibus carrying revellers from the Bailey came upon the crash scene. Matthew Peoples was a passenger on the bus. Through the rain-drenched windows, he saw blue lights flashing in the distance. By this stage, some of the emergency services had arrived and the gardaí had set up a road cordon. When he realised his sister was in the smashed Peugeot, Matthew immediately called home. Terry Peoples answered the phone, half-asleep. 'Rochelle and David were in a bad accident,' Matthew said. On hearing the news, Terry automatically phoned Rochelle and David's mobile phones. Both numbers rang out. He knew then that something was very wrong. Matthew Peoples called home again. This time, he was crying. 'Daddy, they've just covered the car with a blanket. I think Rochelle is dead,' he said.

It was a busy night for Darren Quinn's father, taxi-driver Patrick Quinn. His mobile phone had been ringing, but he never got the chance to pick up. He was dropping off a fare in Buncrana when he came across an unusual sight. His oldest son, Martin, was standing in the middle of the street, crying. 'Martin told me Darren was in an accident,' Patrick recalls. 'That was the first I heard. We drove out to the crash scene. About a mile from the accident, a white Mercedes pulled up. The driver rolled down the window and told me not to bother driving on as the road was closed. "It's a mess," he said. I was determined to get to the accident. I had to see my son.' Patrick Quinn drove as far as the Garda cordon, where he inquired after Darren. 'I'm afraid your son is dead,' a garda said. With these words, Martin Quinn, who was standing beside his father, collapsed on the tarmac. 'We carried him into a nearby house. The woman was very good to us,' Patrick says. 'I went back out to see the car. It was completely smashed up with a blanket thrown over it. I was relieved that Darren had not come out of that car alive, because he would have been no more than a vegetable, lying in a corner for the rest of his life, and I didn't want that for him. I asked the Guard to tell me about the crash. It was only then that I learned there were four more lying in the wreckage alongside Darren.'

Rose O'Connor was asleep when she woke to the sound of someone tapping with a key against her bedroom window. Outside, her sister was trying to wake her up without having to ring the doorbell. Moments later, Rose noticed the lights of a car thrown across the driveway. 'I opened the door to my sister who said, "Charlene was in an accident". A patrol car had just pulled up. I thought, "this will be all right". Charlene probably has broken legs, arms and will need stitches. I wasn't frantic. I wouldn't allow myself to think anything worse. But two Guards knocking on your door at that time of night only have one type of story to tell. I was told my daughter, my beautiful Charlene, my first-born, was dead.'

When Gavin's parents, Annette and Brendan Duffy, learned about the crash, they immediately travelled to the scene. There, they met with Rose and Anthony O'Connor and Pauline and Darren Quinn. Terry and Rosemarie Peoples chose not to visit the crash scene, as did David Steele's father, Ivan. By then, the five bodies had been cut out of the wreckage by fire crews. Bits of cars were strewn all over the road; the scene was reminiscent of a bomb site. There was little noise except for the muffled weeping of those present. A garda asked Annette to identify some of the bodies. 'Charlene and David were lying in the back of one ambulance,' Annette says. 'Charlene, God love her, was just staring ahead with her mouth open. I will always remember her beautiful white teeth. I closed her eyes and mouth. David looked very peaceful, like he was sleeping. My Gavin was cut out of the car last. He left the scene in a coffin in the back of a hearse.'

Rose O'Connor recalls, 'I left my daughter into town that night to meet Gavin. The next time I saw her was in the back of an ambulance at Quigley's Point, with a blanket up to her neck.' The five young people died instantly owing to multiple injuries sustained in the crash. Apart from a few facial cuts and bruises, their bodies showed no major outward signs of trauma. 'Rochelle had only a few cuts. She looked fine. There was no blood on her clothes. They all died innocent,' says Rosemarie Peoples. Patrick Quinn has kept the clothes his son was wearing on the night he died. 'I still have Darren's clothes. There was blood splattered across them. I know because I had to wash the blood out.'

At the turn-off for the Inishowen Peninsula, I notice a road sign in the shape of a coffin with the words *Speed Kills, Kills, Kills*. I consider the warning a timely reminder to motorists driving north along some of the country's most notoriously dangerous roads. The highways of Donegal have claimed so many lives, the county has earned a reputation as a road-safety black spot. Despite clear disadvantages, such as the remote location, and the oftentimes poor road and weather conditions, in the majority of cases, it is still driver error that is to blame for road deaths. 'Brendan Henderson is to blame for the death of our children, but it seemed like it was our children who were initially blamed for causing the crash,' says Annette Duffy. It is four years since the horrific crash that claimed the lives of the five friends from Buncrana, and I've come to meet their parents on a wet, windy day in October 2009. They have had to wait almost four years to see justice done, but at no stage did they give in. 'We had to fight to clear our children's names. No one else could do it for them,' says Terry Peoples. 'We had to see Brendan Henderson go to jail.'

In the days following the crash, the general assumption was that a group of young people en route back from a nightclub must have been driving irresponsibly. Community leaders in Buncrana appealed for action, urging people to get together in an effort to tackle the ongoing problem of young people dying on the roads. The town mayor, Padraig Mac Lochlinn said that communities in Inishowen and across Donegal had been shocked by the deaths. 'After the funerals we are going to have to sit down, examine what responses we're going to take, and what initiatives we need to undertake to address this ongoing tragedy. We can't continue to bury our young people without doing something to tame the circumstances surrounding such deaths.' At the funeral masses of cousins Darren Quinn and Gavin Duffy, Father Con McLaughlin said, 'Since coming to Buncrana, I have witnessed too many young people's bodies lifted from car wrecks and tried to offer consolation to grieving families. Another horrific road crash, another tragedy for Buncrana, and the revival in people's minds of the tragedies that have already taken place in this area. A community stunned by it all asks why, so this morning again could I appeal to young people to just try to be more aware and to understand the dangers which often seem hidden to them but are very real nonetheless.' Father Eddie McGuinness, who officiated at Rochelle's funeral, also asked young people in the congregation to think about why so many crashes were happening.

'At the time of the funerals, there were a lot of young people who wanted to walk out of the church because of this preaching. They felt their friends were automatically being blamed. The parish priest apologised to us afterwards, when all the facts were revealed,' says Brendan Duffy. His son Gavin was the driver of the car. 'The Guards reassured us Gavin was sober. He had always been against drinking and driving. It was very important to us that the rest of the families stuck by us. We had to clear his name.'

There was a lengthy Garda investigation into the crash, and it took the Director of Public Prosecutions almost three years to reach a decision on whether or not to prosecute Brendan Henderson. 'We were left waiting for answers,' says Rosemarie Peoples. 'We threatened to go to Dublin to demand a response from the DPP, but the gardaí said we would be wasting our time. It was very difficult. We had so much anger. We didn't want to be angry, but it's human nature. We knew that Brendan Henderson was at fault, and he was sitting up in Derry and our five children were lying in cold graves. It slowed the grieving process down, making the pain so much harder to endure,' says Rosemarie Peoples.

Her husband, Terry, agrees. 'It was like being up against a brick wall. We were warned not to go to the media. The gardaí put pressure on us to cancel our plans to talk to the press. The delay by the DPP caused us to think that there was not enough evidence to convict Brendan Henderson. We were told that if there was no case we would get our say at the inquest. What good would that be? We wanted a court case. The longer the delay, the worse it looked for our innocent children.'

Eventually, in January 2008, after three Christmases without their loved ones, the Buncrana families held a press conference, demanding an update from the DPP about the investigation into the tragedy. They called on the DPP to decide urgently if there was to be a criminal prosecution in the case. The families believe that this exposure helped to move the process along.

On 15 April 2008, Brendan Henderson, from Derry, was charged with dangerous driving, causing the deaths of the five friends, before Carndonagh District Court in County Donegal. Brendan Henderson, who sat in a wheelchair for the hearing, pleaded not guilty to the charge. The court was told that the delay in bringing charges relating to the crash was because the accused had suffered serious injuries and had been hospitalised for a long time.

The trial got under way at Letterkenny Circuit Court in February 2009, when Brendan Henderson dramatically changed his plea to guilty. The presiding judge, John O'Hagan, said, 'No doubt there will be a certain amount of closure in that someone has admitted responsibility for what happened.' Afterwards, the families expressed surprise and relief, calling it a good day for their children's memory. But it was not until Brendan Henderson was sentenced on 7 May 2009 that the families achieved a proper sense of closure. He was given four years in prison for dangerous driving causing the deaths of the five young people. The court heard that Brendan Henderson had no recollection of the crash, which happened at 3.15 a.m. He had been at a function and had been drinking from 6.30 p.m. in the evening. For some unknown reason, he did not stay in the hotel he had booked into but drove back towards Derry. Superintendent James Coen, who headed up the investigation into the crash, stressed that the young people were totally blameless in the crash. Judge John O'Hagan said: 'Brendan Henderson fractured his spine in three places and is now almost permanently confined to a wheelchair. He will suffer for the rest of his life, both physically and mentally. Each side has been handed down a life sentence, the families for the loss of their children and Henderson has to live with what he did: he killed five people.'

Brendan Henderson apologised to the victims' families in court. 'His apology was too little too late,' says Brendan Duffy. 'He kept quiet for two and a half years, putting us through hell. It was tough having to wait to clear Gavin's name. He could have sent an apology through the local parish priest or the gardaí. A few lines in a letter would have been enough.'

Patrick Quinn feels the same. 'Brendan Henderson's brother-in-law was married to my niece. I saw him years ago, at that family wedding. He was a very tall man who appeared friendly. He was connected to our family in that way, but he never apologised to us – not until he was in front of a judge.'

Rose O'Connor believes Brendan Henderson should have been jailed for longer. 'I hate Brendan Henderson. He was a very silly man to do what he did. My daughter

Charlene can't be replaced, no matter what I do, if I have more children, or I don't, she can't be replaced. I go to her grave every day; Charlene's name engraved in a headstone. Our children were killed in the prime of their lives, through no fault of their own. I don't think Brendan Henderson will ever fully realise what he has done. There were five precious children killed in that car and he didn't even get a year for every life. He'll never know the loss we suffer in our homes. He'll never know the feeling of a lonely house on Christmas morning. Everything is in front of you all of the time. I've five other children who have to get married and have children, and I'll always think about what Charlene and Gavin would have done for their wedding. Charlene's cousin's wedding is coming up. She would have been bridesmaid. The loss is constant. It never leaves you. Brendan Henderson has a daughter. If he was to lose her in the same way, how would he deal with his pain? When your child dies, a part of you dies with them. A part of everybody in the family goes with them. We can't even talk about Charlene because it always leads to tears.'

Rosemarie Peoples rarely thinks about Brendan Henderson any more. 'He is the man who took away our daughter. He is the man who brought devastation to our door. Our home is a lonely place now. I try to get on with things, but I always miss her. We can go out for dinner on a Sunday as a treat, and I feel her loss. We come back to the house and Rochelle is not there. There is no end to it and there never will be. I'm getting on, I have to: if I stop, what will happen to everybody else? But that doesn't mean I'm better or that I'll forgive him. If drunken drivers saw the devastation in homes, they wouldn't drink and drive. I wonder how that man sleeps in his bed at night knowing that he killed five young people.'

Charlene O'Connor, Gavin Duffy, Darren Quinn and Rochelle Peoples are buried side by side in Cockhill Cemetery, Buncrana, while David Steele's grave is in nearby Green Bank Cemetery, Quigley's Point. 'I'd like Brendan Henderson to visit the graves when he gets out of prison,' Annette Duffy says. 'I'd like him to see that reality. I have eight other children, but it doesn't matter if you have eight or one, your family is fractured forever. Our aim was to clear Gavin's name as the driver. He would turn in his grave if he thought people believed he was to blame for the crash. He was anti-drink-driving. Brendan Henderson was secondary to us. I'm glad justice was done. I haven't thought about the man since the day he was put away.'

The inquest into the five deaths took place in Donegal in August 2009. A jury brought in a verdict of death due to injuries sustained in a road traffic crash. Gavin Duffy, Charlene O'Connor, Darren Quinn and Rochelle Peoples, from Buncrana, and David Steele from Quigley's Point all died instantly on impact when hit by Brendan Henderson's car. A blood sample taken from Brendan Henderson in Derry's Altnagelvin hospital showed that he was two and a half times over the legal alcohol limit. Coroner Dr John Madden said, 'Gavin Duffy was nowhere near the legal limit. He was as sober as a judge and no blame could be attached to him or the four passengers. There is no way the five friends could have survived that accident. Death would have been instantaneous, such was the ferocity and severity of the injuries they all suffered.' Superintendent Jimmy Coen told the inquest, 'Gavin Duffy's driving on the night in question and when he overtook Mr McKinney was totally proper. He was an insured named driver for Mr Steele's car. The level of responsibility they showed was in marked contrast to that shown by Brendan Henderson. Their speed at the time of impact was under the speed limit. The speed of the Mazda was over the speed limit – between 93 and 111 kilometres per hour.' Dr Madden closed the inquest. In summary, he said, 'The death of these five young people more than any other accident in Donegal had touched the population in a way that was totally different. It was an awful example of stupidity and drunk-driving. We hear the trite phrase, a waste of life – this truly was. I hope [the inquest] brings some closure to the families and they can now get on with the rest of their lives.'

Each of the families wants to remember their loved ones as they last saw them alive. Patrick Quinn joked with Darren to be good. 'He just smiled back at me, and off he went,' he says. In a gesture that he never used before, Gavin Duffy saluted his parents as he walked out of the house. Charlene O'Connor was bursting with pride over her academic achievements as she got ready to go out. 'Study didn't come easy to her,' says Rose; 'she worked very hard for her independence. She also had a part-time job in a local supermarket.' Rochelle Peoples was looking forward to sleeping in. Her bedroom was being redecorated. 'She never got to see the new carpet in her room, which she had chosen the day before she died,' says Terry. He speaks highly of her boyfriend, David Steele. 'He was a quiet, well-mannered boy. He was a Manchester United Fan. We still let him stay over with us, even though this is a Liverpool house!'

That fateful night, the five friends left their homes in the Inishowen Peninsula, never to return. The families say they are grateful to have each other. Since the deaths of their children, who were so close in life, they, too, have developed strong friendships. 'They all died together,' says Annette Duffy. 'For us, there is a great comfort in knowing that they died while out enjoying life, having a laugh together.'

Brendan Henderson is in Castlerea Prison. Both he and his wife, Marie, who lives in the family home, refused to be interviewed for this book. Marie Henderson declined to comment, except to say, 'the last four years have been hell for our family because of the media. At this stage, we have nothing more to say.'

11

INTENSIVE TERROR

'*My mouth was full with tiny beads of glass that I thought were broken teeth.*' Lorcan Leavy.

Approaching the slipway from the new bypass onto the old road . . . a sharp turn . . . change down the gears. A lorry drives towards him, a big lorry, negotiating the other half of the slipway. Both straighten up, driving towards each other . . . and then it happens . . . the trailer jackknifes, swinging over into his half of the road. Steer to the left to avoid impact. Too late . . . bang!

The sudden impact was deafening, drowning out the sound of Bruce Springsteen on the CD player. Retired schoolteacher Lorcan Leavy remembers darkness in the seconds after the crash, and then stars. The father of six, from Charlestown in County Mayo, could not believe his Nissan people carrier had been hit. 'I noticed that the tail end of the trailer was starting to shudder and move towards me. I swung as far left as I could go. I was convinced I had gone far enough, that I was safe. But the trailer hit the car over the front right wheel, and practically stripped the side out of the car, ripping my arm and my chest,' he says.

The crash happened on 17 July 2007 on a slip road off the Charlestown bypass in County Mayo. He opened his eyes to a scene of twisted metal and broken glass. The five-month-old car was a wreck. Lorcan's mouth was full of tiny beads of glass that he thought were broken teeth. He began to spit them out. Bruce Springsteen continued to sing on the stereo as the wipers tried to wipe a windscreen that no longer existed. Lorcan attempted to turn off the wipers, but found his right arm would not respond. Breathing was difficult; he could only manage short gasps. Lorcan figured he had broken a rib. Checking for further damage, he started at his toes and worked his way up through every joint, muscle and bone, testing and flexing as he went. 'Everything seemed to be in working order except for my right arm and the red-hot sensation on the right side of my chest,' he recalls. Blood trickled down his face into his eyes and mouth. He decided not to move and to wait for help. He remembers thinking about the sheer annoyance at the inconvenience of the crash. 'My mentality at that stage was that it was a near miss. I thought he nearly got me, not realising that he *had* got me.'

Within a short space of time, a salesman arrived on the scene. He immediately reached into the wreckage to turn off the engine. A young nurse from Beaumont Hospital then came across the crash, and took control of the situation until the emergency services arrived. Lorcan stayed sitting in the car. 'The floor was full of glass. Lumps of flesh were gone from my arms. It crossed my mind that I must clean the car. Blood was splattered everywhere, as if someone had squirted a washing-up liquid bottle full of a red liquid all over the place. I noticed what looked like little blobs of porridge. I could not figure out where it had come from. It was only afterwards that I discovered it was my flesh. A large chunk of my arm muscle had exploded and splattered everywhere,' says Lorcan.

A screaming siren signalled to Lorcan that help had arrived. 'The boys from Charlestown are here; we'll soon have you out,' a fire officer told Lorcan. The crew assessed the situation, preparing their equipment. Lorcan recognised one of the men. Never had he been so grateful to see a former pupil. Disorientated and in a state of shock, Lorcan told the fire officers not to cut him out. He insisted he could step out. 'I didn't want them to use a cutter on my nice new car, even though the car was a wreck. I was not thinking straight.' Lorcan was removed from the car and put on to a stretcher. He does not recall any great distress, but has been told by a local garda that he was in fact howling out in pain. 'I remember fleeting snatches – the pain in my chest when the ambulance hit a pothole, the instant of concern when someone cut my shirt off me with a scissors,' he says.

In Mayo General Hospital, Castlebar, a decision was made to attempt to save Lorcan's arm, even though it had initially appeared to be beyond saving. He was bleeding internally, had four broken ribs and a collapsed lung. 'My blood pressure had fallen right down. The doctors had to fight to keep me alive for a number of days. I was put on a ventilator. Saving my life became the priority.' In the course of a fortnight, Lorcan had several surgeries for repair work on his arm. He was transferred to University College Hospital Galway where further orthopaedic and plastic surgery took place.

He fell into an induced coma that was to last for ten days. Those ten days would feel like forever. During that time, he found it difficult to differentiate between dreams and reality. At first, he had benign dreams – his mother was there, stroking his blood-soaked hair. He saw his adult children as children again. His dreams were vivid and clear. 'I dreamed with total clarity that I was put on board a military plane and flown to Moscow for surgery and then flown back to Galway. It took quite a lot of time and effort on the part of my family to convince me that this had not happened.'

Lorcan then entered into a phase where the dreams were no longer benign. 'As I drifted into a state of deep unconsciousness and then on to fretful wakefulness and all of the stages in between, I experienced depths of dementia and paranoia that were terrifying in their intensity. In my deep unconscious state I imagined myself to be in a huge cave-like place, the darkness of the concave roof relieved by myriad images of grotesque faces and people who leered and sneered at my helplessness and distress. These images changed incessantly as they flitted across the darkened sky over my head, always ugly and full of threat. There was background music, a constant shrieking scream on a loop. And far below all this mayhem was a surging flood of multicoloured viscous evil-smelling liquid through which I had to swim, sometimes submerged and gasping for breath, other times swimming on the surface, but never able to rest, always gasping, always struggling. I'm sure my broken ribs and collapsed lung were at the root of my breathing difficulties.' But what about all the other images? Lorcan wondered if he was dead. He asked himself if this was this hell. Had he sinned once too often? He feared his suffering would never end.

Over the next eight days he was kept under sedation to facilitate surgery and to protect him from pain. 'I may have regained consciousness from time to time because I have some memories of people coming and going. Each time I returned to a near-conscious state, my fevered mind took the realities that I could vaguely see around me, and created another version of hell. My mind concocted an elaborate scenario in which the hospital and all the staff were not real; rather, they were clones created by a mastermind nurse, who, for reasons unclear had decided that I would never escape from this surreal, virtual world. In my paranoia I regarded all the staff as the enemy and I treated them with great suspicion.'

Apart from the dementia of deep unconsciousness and the paranoia of near consciousness, a third scenario added to his torment – hallucinations. Lorcan saw things and people who were not there. He saw parked cars outside the glass door of his room. The walls appeared not to be solid. They were made of white, translucent, gauze-like material behind which he could see sinister figures moving menacingly. One of these was a ferocious-looking Samurai character in full armour carrying a double-bladed axe. 'Most frightening of all was a drunken lout with a head of wild hair and a shaggy beard. He wore a scruffy cowboy suit complete with a Stetson hat and high boots. This man hung around outside my room, peering in and even trying to push his way into the room. When two nurses went out to usher him away, I saw him attack them repeatedly with a pickaxe handle until they were both unconscious and bloody. Imagine my amazement and confusion when they both appeared at my bedside later on, looking neat and tidy in their clean, crisp uniforms.'

For two weeks, Lorcan's wife, Una, rarely left her husband's side. As Lorcan began to regain consciousness, he gradually became aware of the presence of the nurses and his family. After ten days, he woke up but showed no great excitement on seeing his wife and best friend. 'He opened his eyes,' recalls Una, 'and I thought this is the longest time in my life since we met that we haven't spoken, and I was so thrilled to see him wake up. But he barely looked or spoke to me.'

Lorcan was extremely paranoid. He told Una that she had to leave the hospital grounds. 'If you don't leave now, you'll be trapped as well,' he said. His dementia and hallucinations were still there. His awareness of the presence of real people came and went as he slipped back into the surreal world of horror, which had become the norm for him.

'By opening and closing my eyes, I drifted from the world of dementia into the world of paranoia and back again. I noticed that when I closed my eyes, it took about ten seconds for the demons to appear – the same when I opened them. So by closing my eyes and counting to ten and then opening them and again counting to ten, I managed to fool the madness and to get some vestige of peace and rest,' says Lorcan. The comfort of his wife's voice was another tool he used to survive the torment.

'I knew he was paranoid and frightened and having horrible hallucinations,' says Una. 'I was expecting a certain amount of distress after numerous operations, anaesthetics and strong medication, but nothing like the extent that he was showing. My biggest fear was that he had a brain injury. But the MRI scan showed he had no head injury. One doctor told me it was the after-effects of the accident, combined with the morphine. I remember one very bad night when he was extremely distressed and completely disorientated. He told me he wanted to lie down. I told him that he was lying down, but he was convinced he was vertical. He kept asking me which way is up. He was so frightened. He kept looking at the ceiling. I told him to look at me. I kept talking to him.'

Una brought in poetry the pair had learned at school. She recited psalms from prayer booklets. She spoke about their life together, the people they were going to meet and the things they would do when he got better. Lorcan, fearful and fretful in the bed, hung on to her every word, listening to the sweet cadence of her voice. Maybe this could save him. He was okay as long as Una kept talking.

'I talked all night, I had to stand up and lean over him. One of nurses brought me in a cup of tea, and as I was going to drink it, Lorcan told me to keep talking. I told him to give me a chance to put the tea in my mouth. My mouth was so dry. He could not get his head around time or days either. I had to write down things for him. One card read "the accident happened on Tuesday, July 17". I had to give him pieces of paper to root him in reality.'

For days, Lorcan had bits of paper in his hands, trying to hold on to reality. During one particularly traumatic 48-hour period, he pulled out all the tubes to which he was attached, disregarding any consequences. Staff attempted to calm him down, immediately hooking him up to his drips again. He shouted at a nurse who had come in to take a blood sample. 'I told her that she was going to pump something into me, I kept saying "no, get away from me with your needle". My arm was in a cast. I still managed to push her away. I was so weak I could hardly move, but I still managed to stop her.'

Probably the most frightening stage for Lorcan was when he was beginning to get a grip on reality. His mind was starting to recover. He could see himself thinking in a paranoid way, but was unsure how to stop it. He heard imaginary music and hollered at the staff to turn the music down. He asked to see a psychiatrist, and talked through his experiences with him. He was told that his mind was reacting to the drugs and the trauma of the road crash and subsequent surgeries. Two weeks after the crash, Lorcan, who until then had had difficulty sleeping, closed his eyes. 'I asked the nurse what time it was. She said it was midnight. After what appeared like minutes later she came into the room again and I asked her the same question. "Three o'clock," she said. I realised I had slept soundly and without nightmares for three hours. I felt marvellous.' I asked the astonished nurse could I have tea and toast for breakfast. "I will get it for you myself before I go off duty," she said. And true to her word she did – the nicest meal I have ever tasted, even though I had a broken tooth, which wiggled about precariously with every bite.'

From that morning on, Lorcan has never looked back. He has required further surgery on his arm, had numerous skingrafts, X-rays, and metal plates put in place. His arm is disfigured and scarred, and has limited strength and mobility, but it still works. He never again experienced delirium, hallucinations or paranoia. He was discharged from hospital on 3 August 2007. After a visit to his GP, Lorcan learned that he had been suffering from Intensive Care Unit syndrome (ICU) or Intensive Care Unit psychosis.

'My experiences of delirium, hallucinations and paranoia are relatively common for people in very stressful and traumatic situations which require a heavy drug regime. It is known as ICU syndrome, a condition which manifests itself in any or all of the experiences I went through,' he says. 'While it undoubtedly was the most terrifying experience of my life, I now know that it does pass and has to be seen as a small price to pay for the intensive care treatment which saved not only my arm, but my life.'

Before his crash, Lorcan had never heard of ICU syndrome. Had he known of the condition in advance, he believes it would have been easier to deal with. 'I kept saying to myself, I can take losing my arm, or even my legs, but I thought if I don't get my peace of mind back, I won't be able to cope for the rest of my life. I think a lot of people are embarrassed when they go through ICU syndrome. No one wants to admit that their mind is gone, but it is more common than we think, and road crash victims can suffer from this.'

'I feel very lucky,' says Lorcan. 'I should not be as good as I am. Most of the muscles in my arm are gone. In reality, I should not be able to play my saxophone or work in the garden, all of the things I used to do prior to my accident. The fact that I survived the crash still amazes me. It was definitely touch-and-go there for a while. When a truck jack-knifes, there is normally only one winner. The colossal weight of the trailer should have blitzed my car. I am grateful that things worked out so incredibly well.' Nowadays Lorcan welcomes the sheer boredom of normality, because he knows that, once lost, normality can be difficult to find again.

12

UNDER THE SURFACE

'We had a wake and Santa Claus on the same night.' Kathleen Gallagher

When Santa Claus came to the Gallagher home in Askill on Achill Island, County Mayo, seven-year-old Catherine wondered why he didn't leave a present for her big sister, Ashling. But Ashling Gallagher's body was lying in a coffin in the living room next to the family tree. Unopened gifts lay scattered under the tinsel-dressed boughs. It was December 2004, the year Christmas stopped for Tommy and Kathleen Gallagher. Three days before Christmas, their daughter, 22-year-old Ashling, was killed in a road traffic crash.

'We had a wake and Santa Claus on the same night,' says Kathleen. 'Catherine was unsure of what was going on. She would look into the coffin and see somebody else. She denied it was Ashling. It is how a child's mind works, not wanting to believe it.'

None of the Gallagher family could accept that Ashling was gone. One of four children, Aisling was extremely close to her siblings, 23-year-old Anita, 20-year-old Martin, and 7-year-old Catherine, the baby of the family, for whom she held an especially soft spot. The legal affairs studies graduate had just completed a four-year degree course at Letterkenny Institute of Technology. There, she met her boyfriend of two years, soldier Chris Murray. The couple were to fly to New York on St Stephen's Day to enjoy New Year's Eve celebrations in the Big Apple. Instead, it was the day she was buried. Ashling was on her way to the bank to collect dollars for the trip when the fatal crash happened.

'She left Achill Island in her red van, glamorous as you like,' says Kathleen. 'I had bought new make-up the day before and I knew she was wearing it. There was a beautiful sheen to her skin. I said, "I bet that's my new make-up you've on," and she said, "Sure you wouldn't mind me using a bit, Mam." No matter what I had, she'd have her fingers stuck in, trying out my products. I told her it really suited her. She looked so beautiful, her hair tied back in a bun, totally and utterly glam. She was going to Castlebar to the bank. Her dollars were ordered and ready for collection. Tommy and I had given her cash for the holiday. She was bursting with excitement about New York. Ashling loved to shop. She spent every last cent on clothes and shoes. She was so into her style.'

Before leaving the house, Ashling texted her father to thank him for the spending money. She then drove towards the N59 Castlebar road in the family Volkswagen van.

Ashling had been driving since she was seventeen years old. Her family say she was a cautious driver who never took risks on the road.

Housewife Kathleen Gallagher waved her daughter off before tidying up the kitchen. Standing at the sink, she soaked the breakfast dishes. Outside, the Atlantic Ocean stretched as far as the eye could see. It was a damp, grey morning; black clouds hovered on the horizon. Whatever the weather, Kathleen had always loved the view from her kitchen window, the toss and turn of the tide down below, and the seagulls swooping in and out of the waves. It was as she gazed out that an extremely lonesome feeling enveloped her without warning. Her eyes welled up with tears. She was suddenly short of breath, and could feel her heart pounding in her chest. Each beat hurt. What's wrong with me, she thought. I shouldn't be like this so close to Christmas. Kathleen wept to herself, unable to shake the uneasy sentiment. She decided to call a friend for a chat. A friendly voice was what she needed. After a short conversation, Kathleen felt a little better, and made some coffee. As it brewed, she inhaled the rich aroma, and continued on with her household chores, sweeping the floor and wiping down the countertop. It was now after twelve noon, and Ashling Gallagher had been dead for twenty minutes. 'Three months after Ashling died, I checked the itemised phone bill,' Kathleen says. 'I discovered that I had called my friend just after Ashling crashed. That unbearable, lonely, sad feeling came upon me at the exact time my daughter left this world. There was a reason for my having been so upset. It wasn't just by chance. The message was being sent to me somehow that she had died.'

Ashling was killed when her van skidded on the road at a bad bend just outside the village of Mulranny on the N59. It is believed she applied the brakes as she rounded the bend, travelled across the road and collided with an oncoming cement lorry. She died at the scene from her injuries. At the time, Mayo County Council was carrying out resurfacing works on a 2-kilometre stretch along the road. Tommy Gallagher claims that the road surface where Ashling crashed was a temporary surface called Dense Bitumen Macadam (DBM). 'Dense Bitumen Macadam is not designed or manufactured to be used as a running surface, but rather to give a road shape and strength,' he explains. 'Tar and chips is the surface dressing which provides skid resistance.' He maintains that there were no warning signs indicating a temporary surface or speed restrictions in the 100 km/h zone on the day of the crash. Mayo County Council disputes Mr Gallagher's claims, insisting that two warning signs were in place, along with traffic cones.

Following the tragic incident, the National Roads Authority wrote to Mr Gallagher confirming that the surface of the section of road where Ashling died did not comply with requirements for a permanent road. Mayo County Council had plans to cover the road with a surface dressing containing tar and chips, but postponed this because of the time of year and poor weather conditions. In December 2009, Mayo County Manager, John Condon, said that the council accepts no liability for the crash. He refused to comment further on the case, but speaking to the *Irish Independent* in March 2005, he said, 'I don't believe this road is dangerous. We don't agree with Mr Gallagher's analysis and interpretation. We believe other factors may have been involved.' Tommy Gallagher still maintains that there are serious flaws in the management of Ireland's non-national roads, and has been campaigning on this issue since his daughter's death.

Shortly after the crash, Kathleen Gallagher noticed the priest's car drive by the house. 'I figured they must be making Christmas house calls, visiting the sick and elderly. The car then reversed and backed into our driveway. I go to Mass every Sunday. They were hardly coming to see me. I thought they must want directions,' she recalls. 'The two priests came to the front door. With very serious faces, they told me that there had been an accident. I immediately asked, "Was it Ashling?" When they answered, "Yes", I knew it had to be bad. Why else would there be two of them? I was waiting for them to tell me that she had to be airlifted to Beaumont Hospital. I asked, "How bad is it?" The Parish Priest said, "It's bad, Kathleen. She didn't make it." Kathleen's legs went from under her and she grabbed hold of the porch door to steady herself. Kathleen was conscious of the fact that Catherine was running around in the kitchen, counting the hours until Santa arrived. She had to pull herself together for the sake of her seven-year-old daughter. Her husband, Tommy, was at work in Dublin. Kathleen phoned him with the devastating news, but he refused to believe her. 'He told me I was a liar. I had to give the phone to the priest. I could hear Tommy roaring and shouting down the phone to the priest. The priest had to go out the back of the house, trying to calm him and convince him of what had just happened.'

Construction supervisor Tommy Gallagher was working near Heuston Station when his mobile phone rang. He was planning to finish his shift early. He had €200 cash in his pocket and had decided to give Ashling some extra money for her trip to America. It would be just between them. He would go to the bank before it closed. After his conversation with the priest, Tommy called Ashling's phone over and over again. It kept ringing out. He kept dialling. Ashling was the most cautious of his four children. She never put herself in any danger. Even in childhood, when going out to play, she would be the one who would check if she needed her coat. It was an instinctive trait, to be vigilant. She was a careful driver, the most wary of his three children who drove. It was simply not possible that she had crashed, that she was dead. Tommy phoned his son Martin, who was working on another building site in Dublin. The two men travelled to a nearby relative's house. Tommy's cousin would later drive them on the long, lonely journey home to Achill. But Tommy was unable to move. For hours, he sat in an armchair in the corner of the sitting room, staring straight ahead of him, saying nothing. 'No one could move me,' he says. 'They tried to coax me out to the car. I was in a total state of shock, a statue. I could not hear anyone or anything. We didn't leave for Achill until very late in the evening. It took me at least three hours to realise that I had to move, that I had to go home. I arrived back at the house around midnight.'

Kathleen had been surrounded by family and friends all day. She was distraught. Crippled with grief, she asked her sister to drive her to the local Garda station that evening. A young garda was on duty on the desk. Kathleen approached the hatch, threw her arms into the air and started to scream at the garda, demanding to know what exactly had happened, why her daughter had crashed. 'I just took a notion,' she says. 'Looking back now, I was insane with grief.

I think the poor garda was so frightened. I must have seemed like a mad woman. He probably thought I was going to attack him.'

The following day, Tommy and Kathleen made the journey to the morgue at Mayo General Hospital in Castlebar. Ashling's face was covered in lacerations and bruises. Her parents did not recognise her at all. 'The morgue attendants were whispering in my ear, preparing me for what I was about to encounter, telling me to brace myself,' says Kathleen. 'I didn't know my own daughter. I still have serious flashbacks of Ashling in the morgue. But I'm glad I saw her. Why would I turn my back on her? When it comes to the crunch, you face it.' Kathleen's biggest regret is that she didn't go to the morgue sooner. 'My two sisters, Pauline and Rose, saw her on the day she died, shortly after the accident. Ashling was still warm. Once I knew my own people had seen her, I felt relieved. I didn't think my poor baby was left so alone. I wanted to go to see her, but was advised not to. I think that every hour that went by, the bruising worsened; she deteriorated. In hindsight, the one thing I will regret until the day that I die is not having gone to see her that first day. I should have gone. Because when I did eventually go to pick her up, I didn't know her.'

Tommy Gallagher wanted the people who loved Ashling to be able to say goodbye, and so decided on an open coffin for the wake. Ashling wore a wedding veil across her disfigured face. Kathleen was unsure about the open coffin. She thought it might be best to have it closed during the day and open only at night, when the family were alone. Tommy believes that would not have worked. 'Ashling was a very popular girl,' he explains. 'She worked in a hotel in

Achill for three summers. She studied for four years in college. She had so many friends. I didn't want Ashling in the sitting room in a closed box. All her friends from college came down. They came from as far as Australia. A coach-load of pals came down from Letterkenny. She was brought to the church on Christmas Day.'

Following her death, Tommy Gallagher approached Mayo County Council in a bid to find out all he could about the road conditions along the N59, where Ashling had died. 'The first time I stood on that stretch of road, I knew exactly what I was standing on. I was standing on Dense Bitumen Macadam. It was the day after the crash. Around ten bouquets of flowers had been left at the spot where Ashling drew her last breath.' Tommy says that he also noticed several new signs had been erected on either side of the crash spot, warning motorists of a slippery surface and bad bends. There were a number of other crashes along the same stretch of road where Ashling crashed. Within weeks of her death, three other drivers lost control. 'Between 12 December 2004 and 23 January 2005, there was one fatal, two write-offs and one near miss,' says Tommy. 'Fortunately, no one was seriously injured in the other accidents.'

After this spate of crashes, Independent Mayo TD Dr Jerry Cowley took an interest in Ashling's case. He called for a national audit of unexplained road deaths and serious crashes to determine if roadworks were in any way responsible. He believes many crashes blamed on driver error are in fact caused by vehicles skidding and going out of control on DBM base course which has not been dressed with tar and chips or hot rolled asphalt. Tommy Gallagher and Dr Cowley TD both spoke out after the Navan school bus crash, which claimed the lives of five teenage schoolgirls in May 2005 – the worst school bus disaster in the history of the State. The crash also happened on an unfinished road surface, similar to the type of road surface where Ashling was killed. Prior to this tragic crash, in January 2005, Tommy Gallagher sent a letter to the then Minister for Transport, Martin Cullen TD, and Bus Eireann highlighting the dangers of temporary road surfaces to school buses. The letter also urged local authorities nationwide to implement measures, including special speed restrictions and warning signs on unfinished roads which remain open for traffic. Both Dr Cowley and Tommy Gallagher are continuing with their road safety campaign.

In November 2009, Tommy and Kathleen Gallagher travelled as part of an Irish delegation to the European Commission in Brussels. The group consisted of two other families, who had lost their daughters in road traffic crashes on regional or local roads. Together, they outlined their frustrations with local authorities, especially with regard to obtaining information. In each case, the families believe the loss of life was partially the result of serious flaws in the management of Ireland's regional and local roads, also known as non-national roads.

Tommy Gallagher told the European Commission his beliefs about Ashling's death – that the road surface and lack of proper signage contributed to her crash. Afterwards, he said, 'For a start, they seemed to be amazed when they heard our submissions, and even more astounded at how long our cases had been going on. They could not understand why we could not get closure on our cases in Ireland. We just want people to know that Ashling was driving on a road that didn't have the right skid resistance. I am looking for transparency and for an independent body to be set up to investigate these accidents and for information to be available to the loved ones of the deceased. We should be entitled to that information. Lots of families simply give up looking for answers, because it is too time-consuming and draining.'

The Farren family also went to Brussels. In 2001, Sean Farren's daughter, Sinéad, was killed in County Donegal when her car went out of control on a newly resurfaced road. She had been married for just two years and, at the time of the crash, was delivering a birthday card to her mother-in-law. Her thirty-first birthday would have been in November 2009. Sean Farren believes he got a fair hearing at the European Commission. 'This is the first time that anyone sat down and listened to anything we had to say. At the time of Sinead's death, a warning sign had fallen over. We believe new signs were put up immediately afterwards.'

In Kerry, in April 2005, 18-year-old Eileen Keane and her 23-year-old boyfriend Trevor Tuite were both killed after their vehicle hit another at an unmarked crossroads. Eileen's father, Richard, travelled to Brussels to have his say. 'They weren't familiar with the road and they followed another driver. There was no signage there and they drove straight out into the road and a minibus hit them. Signage was erected after the accident.' The Keane family said they were particularly annoyed at the difficulty they experienced in obtaining information on their daughter's death and subsequent investigation.

Following the meeting, the European Commission said it would write to the Oireachtas Transport Commitee and to the local authorities in question on behalf of the three families.

Tommy Gallagher says he is pleased with the outcome of the trip to Brussels, but he regrets that he had to go all the way to Europe to get a hearing. 'It's nearly five years since we lost our daughter and we are nowhere, really, with regard to getting answers. Brussels went very well, but we have had to fight every arm of the State and there is nothing there to help us.' The Gallagher family say they will keep fighting for the truth because they believe there is a case to answer. 'We are not denying that Ashling ended up on the wrong side of the road, but she ended up there for a reason; something brought her across. We believe that what Ashling encountered that day was like black ice. A lot of cars can drive through black ice without incident, but one can hit it the wrong way, or at the wrong time. In her case, she had to brake.'

Ashling was five years dead at Christmas 2009. Catherine is now twelve years old, but she talks as if Ashling is still alive. 'She can repeat conversations that they shared, word for word, as if she had just been talking to her yesterday,' says Kathleen. 'They were so close. Ashling went to see Catherine in the school nativity play the day before she died. She was so proud of her baby sister, and always devoted so much time to her. She took her swimming, to the beach, the cinema and shopping. In 2001, I fell ill and had to spend time in Galway Hospital. Ashling had just started her summer job, but gave it up immediately to look after the family. She ran the house for those seven weeks, and never once cribbed or moaned. She was just so utterly devoted; there was a strong bond between them. Catherine used to say that Ashling was not dead, but still out in Mulranny, wandering around lost. She would ask me to take her to the hospital in Castlebar to see if we could find her. "Mammy, we should go and carry out a search. She is in the hospital, but we might not recognise her because she'll be wearing someone else's pyjamas." It broke my heart to hear her say such things.' Now, Catherine sleeps in Ashling's old room, complete with handbags, scarves and boots that used to belong to her older sister. The handbags and scarves are stored at the end of her bed, and in the wardrobe Ashling's favourite outfits hang side by side. 'Catherine likes to keep some of Ashling's things with her,' explains Kathleen. 'I have more of her clothes in a suitcase in my bedroom, and some in the attic. She was a shopaholic. I like to look at her good clothes sometimes. That's why I have them pressed and hanging in the wardrobe. At times, I feel Ashling's presence. I know she is never too far away. When I'm shopping for clothes and find something I want in my size, I feel she is showing it to me.'

Ashling Gallagher's anniversary Mass is held every year on Christmas Eve, in the local church. Kathleen spends the weeks prior to the service buying decorations and festive lighting for the occasion. The bouquets of fresh flowers are ordered well in advance. It is important to Kathleen that the service is perfect. 'The community makes a big effort. Before Ashling died, people went to Christmas Eve Mass. Now they come to Ashling's Mass.'

Afterwards, the Gallagher family visit Ashling's grave. There, under a sea of tiny white stars in the quiet, still night, they lay fresh white lilies, red roses and sprigs of holly on her pebbled graveside, and they speak to her in silence. 'Every year, she does something for us, to let us know that she is listening, that she hears us,' says Kathleen. 'Last year, we went to the grave before the Mass. As the light faded, we were startled by the beautiful array of colours in the sky: pinks, yellows, purple, blues, all the colours you could imagine. There was a warm glow over the island; the sky was smiling down on us as we made our way from the cemetery. Since she died, there are always shooting stars in Achill on Christmas Eve. I remember one year when Catherine thought she saw Santa Claus in the sky. She panicked, and couldn't get back to the house quick enough. She thought Santa would get there before her. But it was a falling star that seemed to take forever to fall.'

13

COLLISION CULTURE

'The only acceptable number of road deaths is zero.' Conor Faughnan.

There is a stereotypical Irish road death which almost always involves young male drivers crashing in the middle of the night. The story goes like this: a group of young people are out for the evening. John is the designated driver. He usually, but not always, stays sober. John, who recently got his full licence, collects his friends. A furry dice dangles from the rear-view mirror as the girls, smelling of cheap perfume, preen themselves in the back seat. They apply shiny lip gloss, looking forward to a night of flirtatious fun in the local pubs and nightclubs. Between the hours of midnight and 5 a.m. the group of friends pile into the car for the drive home. The passengers are drunk, rowdy and loud. John drives back on secondary roads in a rural area. He knows the route extremely well; he has driven it many times at speed. Dance music from the stereo system blasts into the car. John picks up the pace, pressing down on the accelerator. He is driving too fast and – with no other vehicle involved – he loses control on a bend and hits a tree. The result is multiple fatalities. In some cases, he smashes head on into an approaching car.

Despite the huge amount of research and literature on road safety – covering technology, road development, enforcement, social attitudes and education – the single biggest problem Ireland has is talking to John. He is not unique to Ireland. Statistics show that internationally young men are over-represented in road deaths. Certain personality traits may account for this disparity between young male drivers, like John, and other sections of society. John tends to take risks. He ascribes masculine virtues to fast driving. He considers car use as an expression of personal worth; he drives fast to impress peers. John is a Celtic Tiger cub, well educated, confident, and driving since he turned seventeen, when he was, as promised, put on the insurance of the family saloon. With poor public transport in his area, John has always relied on the car to get to where he needed to go, be it to work or to a social occasion. His first trip to the local nightclub was probably as a passenger in his brother's car.

John is not easily shocked. He watched *Pulp Fiction* when he was twelve. He does not avert his eyes from graphic road safety adverts because he is not completely horrified by the images. He joined the social networking site Bebo when he was fourteen. His My Space page displays photos of Ferraris and James Bond's Aston Martin. John upgrades his mobile phone every few months, has 150 channels on his television box set and wireless Internet access. John downloads all the latest music onto his iPod. He plays Gaelic football and follows English soccer. During the week, he attends college in one of the country's main cities. He only vaguely remembers Gay Byrne, who once presented *The Late Late Show*, because his mother was a fan of the broadcaster. Politics do not interest John. When he is asked about road safety, he gives a textbook, socially desirable answer. He knows what people want to hear because he learned it in Transition Year when he was fifteen years old.

Road Safety Expert Conor Faughnan of the Automobile Association of Ireland says, 'Transition Year students, almost without exception, are an extremely good audience on road safety matters. The issue is hugely relevant to this age-group. I recently gave a talk to a Transition Year class in a school in South Dublin. Out of sixty pupils in the class, fifty-five had already been promised that they would be put on the insurance of the family car for their seventeenth birthday. Every group that has done work with Transition Year kids has reported that they are enthusiastic, intelligent and willing.'

John was once one of those students, eager and receptive, but at some stage in the course of the following five years, he tuned out. The challenge is to get John interested in road safety again, and to talk to him in a meaningful way; to convince him that driving safely is 'cool'.

Conor Faughnan believes that clever hooks are required to entice young drivers into becoming more safety conscious. He commends the Road Safety Authority's 2009 radio campaign, which featured the girlfriends of young men asking them to slow down. 'It's possible to devise messages which link safe driving to male virtues,' says Faughnan. 'A young male driver is unlikely to slow down on the road because Gay Byrne says so, but he may well be influenced by his girlfriend. I would like to find a message which says that if you drive fast, if you take risks, then not only are you not cool, you are actually a tosser. Put simply, it should show that bad drivers are sexual failures who boast but can't back it up. Those who drive sensibly are more worldly-wise, intelligent, sophisticated and vastly more successful sexually. I am conscious that we may not know our audience well enough. I'd like to learn more about what they do, where they socialise, what television programmes they watch and when, what travel plans they make. I'd also like to know about their outlook and values, and examine their driving patterns. I believe all of the road safety agencies need to get together for a brainstorming session. We need to question how we can get through to these drivers; what media should we use? Traditional approaches may still work best but I'd like to hear how and if we can use mobile phones, texting initiatives, product placement and celebrity endorsement. We need successful marketing campaigns to reach young adults.'

Speeding

Inappropriate speed is the single greatest contributory factor in road deaths and serious injuries. Over 40 per cent of fatal crashes in Ireland are caused by excessive or inappropriate speed. As the well-known road safety slogan says, 'the faster the speed, the bigger the mess'. A driver is twenty times more likely to die if involved in a crash at 80 km/h, compared to an impact speed of 30 km/h. The impact of a crash when driving at 50 km/h is equivalent to dropping a car from the top of a two-storey building, a 100 km/h impact is equivalent to a fall from eleven storeys, and a crash at 150 km/h equates to a thirty-storey drop. Chief Engineer Harry Cullen of the National Roads Authority (NRA) says, 'You are supposed to drive at a speed that is comfortable for the environment you are in. A lot of people, especially young male drivers, see the speed limit as a target. I should be doing 100 kilometres on this road even though it has twists and severe bends. Potholes are pretty much gone. Potholes won't kill you unless you're driving over them at 100 miles an hour. What will kill you is going too bloody fast. I drive all over the country for my job and have come across hundreds of large skid marks on road surfaces left over from young lads doing doughnuts. This happens at 3 a.m. on a big wide road; you can't traffic-calm that. It's an enforcement issue, but the Guards can't be everywhere. It's like the United States during the 1950s when kids could finally afford cars. Ireland is going through the first generation of people who have cars at the age of seventeen and eighteen.'

The National Roads Authority's primary function, under the Roads Act 1993, is to provide a safe and efficient network of national roads. The independent statutory body maintains all national primary and secondary roads and supervises the construction of any new national routes. Local authorities have responsibility for all other regional and local roads.

The NRA also examines crash data. Together with the gardaí and the Road Safety Authority, it has completed an extensive analysis of the collision history on the road network where speed was a contributory factor. From this information, crash hotspots are identified. 'We call accident black spots a cluster,' explains Harry Cullen. 'If there have been three crashes in any 8-kilometre stretch in a three-year period, then that place is considered a cluster. If a crash rate on a stretch of road is twice the national average, it is also considered a cluster. Because Ireland is such a small country, and owing to the random nature of crashes, we can't get a clear picture looking at one year, so we examine three years of crash data at a time.'

By the end of 2007, the NRA had identified 400 clusters across the country. Once highlighted, road safety engineers are sent to the locations to investigate. 'We ask how we can impact to make the road safer. We have six engineers who visit these sites. First, they file through Garda accident reports to look for patterns. They might find that all of the crashes involve cars turning right. We look for engineering solutions; things like chevrons going around a bend at night time. We have put over 150 traffic calming measures into place at the entrances and exits to villages across Ireland. There are practical solutions, like a line of sight, cutting a hedgerow or getting rid of a curve. But the road is an inanimate object; it is how we behave with it that counts,' says Harry Cullen.

Clusters are also termed 'Collision Prone Zones'. According to the gardaí, these are road sections measuring about 5 to 8 kilometres which have been identified as being predisposed to crashes. Details of these roads can be found on the Garda website. Drivers are encouraged to look them up for their own area. Awareness is central to fighting road carnage.

The Garda National Traffic Bureau (GNTB) was established in 1997 to formulate policy and oversee traffic policing throughout the state. Operational Traffic Corps

Units based in each Garda Division enforce the policies developed by the GNTB. The Bureau chief is Assistant Commissioner Eddie Rock, who says the biggest challenge facing them, and the number one killer on our roads, is speed. Considerable resources have been allocated to traffic policing; the personnel strength of the Traffic Corps (in 2009) stands at 1,082.

'Young men in the seventeen to thirty-four age-group use excessive speed more than any other motorist,' says Commissioner Rock. 'Inexperience and speed are critical elements in most crashes involving young men. Garda resources are being pumped into this problem. We have identified boy racers at a local level. Our members have approached them and their parents. The aim is to target boy racers who go out speeding in the middle of the night. We get our people out at those times. We know the areas in the country where this type of activity happens, and are determined to clamp down on it once and for all. We also know the dangerous roads. A CT68 form must be filled out for every traffic collision reported to us. If speed is found to be a factor, then it is noted on the form and put into our central system. Local communities also inform us about speeding locations. Eighty per cent of our speed enforcement is in those high-risk areas.'

Commissioner Rock rejects criticisms levied at the force about speed traps. 'I would have to absolutely disagree with the view that we are revenue-gatherers. That is not our job. We have a Revenue Commissioner. The motorways are the safest method of travel. There is only a small percentage of our enforcement taking place on the motorways. We are not looking to catch people going five kilometres over the speed limit on a motorway. By early 2010, hundreds of mobile speed cameras will be in place in high-risk locations; areas identified by evidence of speeding. This evidence dictates where they go.'

New enforcement technology has made the job of traffic policing easier. A number of Garda patrol vehicles can now scan thousands of car number plates to ascertain whether or not drivers have paid tax and insurance. A new computer system was fitted to over 100 cars in summer 2009. The device can read plates using a camera and then digitally check their details. It is also useful for speed enforcement. 'The Automatic Number Plate Recognition system (ANPR) is used in patrol cars by many police forces worldwide. It means we can take a more intelligence-led approach to speeding. New cars fitted with this high-tech equipment can read number plates in real time; the information is automatically fed through to our PULSE internal computer system. We can cross-reference numbers against a list provided daily by insurance companies. We know instantly if a car is taxed and insured. We have three vehicles in each division fitted with the device, which scans number plates at around one per second on cars travelling up to 160 kilometres per hour. It cost €750,000 to install but is great value from all perspectives as it also helps in the fight against crime.'

In Ireland, the creation of the penalty points system in November 2002 and the introduction of random breath testing in July 2006 helped change how we drive. The penalty points system brought routine traffic violations into a clearly understood modern format. Good laws induce good behaviour. Suddenly, people drove more carefully, sticking to the speed limit in an effort to avoid points; the death rate fell. This reduction in carnage was an outstanding example of cause and effect. Figures from November 2009 show that while 482,484 people had two penalty points on their licence, the number of people with four or six was much less, and only about 960 motorists had been put off the road for accumulating twelve penalty points since the system was introduced. The yellow card warning system is clearly effective and is part of the new landscape of respect for the enforcement of road safety traffic laws.

Mandatory Alcohol Testing

Good laws are of no value without proper enforcement. The clampdown on speeding eased after the initial introduction of the penalty points system and the death rate rose again in 2004 and 2005. This trend was to change with the creation of Mandatory Alcohol Testing (MAT), which allows the gardaí to breathalyse drivers at checkpoints. The measure, introduced on 21 July 2006, cut immediately through to the public consciousness, making a huge difference overnight in terms of the numbers of people who were willing to take a risk with alcohol.

'While the statute books said it was illegal to drink and drive, there was no real expectation of getting caught,' says Conor Faughnan. 'It has always been a fear of enforcement rather than a road safety issue that persuaded people not to drink and drive.' The new legislation was hailed a success. In 2006, the second lowest number of fatalities on Irish roads in forty-one years was recorded (365), despite the increase in population and number of registered vehicles. The number of drink-driving cases dealt with by the

District Courts rose by 79 per cent in 2006, compared to 2005, i.e., 27,836, up from 15,540 in 2005.

Alcohol is one of the main killers on Irish roads. Legislation such as MAT was urgently needed to help tackle the problem. A study published by the Health Service Executive (HSE), *Alcohol in Fatal Road Crashes in Ireland in 2003*, examined 301 collisions that killed 335 people in 2003. It found that alcohol was a factor in 37 per cent of fatal crashes. A similar study in Australia and Finland revealed that alcohol was a factor in 25 per cent of fatal crashes.

The HSE study also found that driving while drunk is predominantly a male problem. Ninety per cent of drivers whose alcohol consumption was a contributory factor in a fatal crash were male and the highest risk ages were nineteen to thirty-four. Weekends through to Monday morning were found to be the high-risk period for alcohol-related fatal crashes. Sunday is the worst day for road death.

The one simple enforcement measure of random breath-testing has brought about a dramatic improvement, over a remarkably short period, in the drink-driving figures. In 2006, the proportion of those found drink-driving was one in every fifty persons stopped. By 2008, it was one in 200. The strong enforcement countrywide has gone hand in hand with a sharp reduction in road deaths.

Assistant Garda Commissioner Eddie Rock confirmed that the force carried out 563,115 breath tests during 2008. Before random breath testing, that figure was as low as 12,000 per year. 'We have tackled drink-driving very significantly. The MAT legislation made a huge difference to us. When it was first rolled out, many more drivers were testing positive than is the case today. What we have in place now allows us to save lives. Drink-driving crosses all barriers, affecting all sections of society. Prior to MAT, we had to form an opinion before we stopped a car, and then we had to form an opinion that the driver was incapable of driving before we administered any test. The driver may have had the ability to consume alcohol and not be observed to be impaired. We had extreme difficulty in proving our authority, getting people to the station and finally to court. If we could not prove our suspicion, everything else failed. MAT gave us the authority to set up a checkpoint and test each driver in a non-discriminatory manner, and allowed us to get over the issue of justifying our suspicions. People are very receptive to an idea when it is seen to be enforced in a practical way.'

Assistant Commissioner Rock agrees with early morning checkpoints, and says that there has to be a balanced approach to the legislation. 'Mostly, detections and arrests for drink-driving in the morning arise from observations of citizens or an on-duty Guard. Most arrests do not happen at those times. But if a person drinks exceptionally the night before to such an extent that they are incapable of driving the next morning, then they should not be on the road.'

Eddie Rock believes a change in culture has made errant driving behaviour socially unacceptable, particularly drink-driving. 'Many road users have changed their behaviour and this has come about through greater compliance with road traffic laws. However, the Head of the Traffic Bureau admits that the issue of driving under the influence of drugs is not so easy to tackle. 'There is no machine or technical device which helps us to indicate that a person is incapable of driving because of the consumption of drugs. Any prosecution is based around the proof that the person has consumed drugs; the proof of impairment is by way of our evidence. There is a saliva test that is used by the traffic police in Australia, but how does this prove impairment? One could have smoked a joint the night or week before and there would still be traces of the drug in that person's system. Likewise, in Ireland, testing can be done in the Medical Bureau of Road Safety which will give us information regarding the presence of drugs in the body, but that is a long way from proving impairment. How do you get around it? You don't get around it. To prove that the person is incapable of having proper control of the vehicle is extremely difficult. MAT has brought us a long way forward, but we are no different from any other jurisdiction in relation to drugs. If drug use is increasing in society, then it is increasing in driving; one follows the other. It would be hard to think that it would not be a factor in road deaths.'

To aid the gardaí in detection, the new Road Traffic Bill 2009 gives them powers to carry out Preliminary Impairment Tests. These coordination tests will help determine whether a driver is under the influence of an intoxicant, including drugs, and will include tasks such as walking in a straight line. Gardaí will also check for physical signs of intoxication, such as dilated pupils.

Conor Faughnan also believes that Ireland as a country has matured in its attitude towards drink-driving. 'Poor behaviours like speeding and drink-driving are less tolerated now culturally than they would have been in previous years,' he says. 'It is well documented that we had until recently broad social tolerance of drink-driving. It would not have been at all uncommon for people to have a few pints after a round of golf. The rule of thumb was if you were not totally drunk, you had a good chance of being charming to a Guard. If you were stopped, you could talk your way out of it. Specific to Ireland, we have made a dramatic sea change in our attitude towards drink-driving. We have grown up. Ten or fifteen years ago, you could meet someone and with an ironic wink and a laugh, they would tell you stories about driving home drunk and getting away with it. There was almost an element of bravado about it. Nowadays people don't talk like that; you don't admit to cheating on your taxes, you don't admit to slapping your children and you don't admit to drinking and driving. It may still exist as a practice, but it has become totally socially unacceptable.'

Safety Standards

During the 1970s, the worst period for road deaths in Ireland, an average of fifty people lost their lives every month. Annual figures topped 600, despite the fact that there were only between 400,000 and 800,000 cars on the road. When motorcyclist Declan Real crashed in 1979, he was lucky to survive. Declan, from Limerick, remembers just how bad the roads were back then.

'I was twenty-two years of age when I had my accident. I had been working in Dublin for the day and was on my way back home to Limerick. Some parts of the main roads were similar to country lanes, full of twists and turns. I was travelling through County Offaly when the crash happened. I didn't see a tractor and trailer pull out of a field. I hit the tractor and went flying over it.'

Declan was rushed to Nenagh General Hospital in County Tipperary, where he was treated for two broken legs and arms. Fortunately his injuries were not life-threatening, but for decades his leg has continued to give him trouble. He has had to walk with the aid of a stick or crutches and undergo a series of operations to help improve his mobility. Eventually, in 2009, Declan had to have his leg amputated. 'The crash was so long ago, but I've been living with the repercussions of it ever since,' he says.

Ireland's road safety record has improved dramatically since the time of Declan Real's crash. This general trend of improvement is not limited to Ireland. Every developed country has had a similar experience. The United Nations has recently highlighted that road deaths are a larger problem in the developing world than in the OECD countries.

Apart from legislation and enforcement, there are a number of other key reasons for road safety progression, as road safety expert Conor Faughnan outlines, 'The standard of vehicles has improved dramatically with the introduction of new technologies like airbags, crumple zones, anti-lock braking systems and laminated glass. Twenty years ago, a very common type of injury to present as a result of a road traffic crash was the loss of both eyes from flying glass. Nowadays, modern car glass does not shatter, and if it does, it shatters into tiny beads, not shards. Glass technology has prevented and almost entirely removed the injuries that were being caused by flying glass.'

He recalls a personal story, 'My parents were involved in a serious car crash in the Dublin Mountains on their wedding night over forty years ago. Both were injured and hospitalised for a number of months. They survived, lived to tell the tale and procreate. Had they had the exact same incident in a modern car, I believe they would have walked away from it.'

Conor Faughnan also points out that road standards have also improved very significantly. 'Better road infrastructure improves safety. So does increased levels of Garda enforcement and the "social mandate" which is a prerequisite for policing. Attitudes towards drink-driving illustrate this,' he says.

The National Roads Authority claims that Irish roads are three times safer today than they were in the 1970s. Dr Harry Cullen highlights the importance of motorways. He says that Ireland will have 12,000 kilometres of motorway by the end of 2010, linking the five major cities of Dublin, Cork, Limerick, Galway and Waterford. 'From a road safety perspective, motorways and dual carriageways are between seven and ten times safer than single carriageway roads. Every time we get rid of a single carriageway road, we are not going to get head-on collisions with four or five people being killed. Motorway pile ups are much less frequent. We have had only one in ten years, on the N7. The statistics tell the story. A total of 564 people died on the roads in 1980, when there were only around 900,000 cars in the country. In 2005, there were 397 road deaths when the number of registered vehicles stood at 2.1 million,' he says.

Trend in Road Fatalities

Official Garda figures show that, in the 1980s, the number of fatalities was generally in the 500s while in the 1990s that figure fell to the 400s. Despite improvements in the road network and advanced technology in cars, the death toll towards the end of the 1990s increased. The year 1997 was one of the worst for road deaths in recent times. A total of 472 people were killed, or an average of 39 per month. This prompted the government to take action and the first Road Safety Strategy was introduced, a five-year plan to reduce road deaths and injuries. It contained a number of recommendations and the strategy worked. By December 2000, road deaths fell again to an average of 35 per month.

Nine out of ten fatal collisions are caused primarily by the behaviour of road users. This, the RSA say, is a fact consistent over time. Changing the attitudes of road users is one of the biggest challenges facing road safety campaigners. This decade has seen the most positive results in this regard. In 2000 the European Union announced as one of its millennium goals the desire to reduce the annual European road death figure by 50 per cent between 2000 and 2010. All EU countries have committed to this with varying degrees of success.

In 2006 the government established the Road Safety Authority which took over the functions of the National Safety Council. The ultimate aim of the RSA is to save lives. It advises the Minister for Transport, who then develops policy for road safety. The statutory body also has responsibility for driver training and testing. The RSA has produced a Road Safety Strategy 2007–2012, which sets the framework for reducing deaths and injuries on our roads through a series of 126 actions, each to be completed by a target date. So far, substantial progress has been made on the implementation of these goals. Speeding ranks as the number one challenge. It lists the primary causes of road collisions, deaths and injuries as speed, impaired driving (through alcohol, drugs or fatigue), failure to use or properly use seat belts and child safety restraints, and unsafe behaviour towards or by vulnerable road users (pedestrians, cyclists, young children and older people.) The Chairman of the Road Safety Authority, Gay Byrne, says that education is central to tackling speed. 'By 2012, all primary school children will have completed a road safety programme. The RSA continues to work with the Department of Education and Science to develop road safety programmes for schools as part of Transition Year.'

Road deaths may never be eliminated, but they can be reduced. Ireland has improved its road safety record dramatically, but has yet to reach the target goal of best practice countries in Europe. These countries, including the Netherlands, Norway and the United Kingdom, have achieved a reduction to fifty deaths per million of population, and are already committed to improving this position by a further 20 per cent. To be in line with them, Ireland would have to reduce road deaths to about 18 per month or 210 per year.

In 2008, the country came closer than ever to this objective – 279 people died on the Republic's roads, the lowest annual total since records began more than forty years ago. This represents an improvement of 41 per cent from 107 people killed per million inhabitants in 2001 to 63 in 2008. The trend continued into 2009. Likewise, the number of people killed on the roads in Northern Ireland in 2008 was the lowest on record. In recent years, the trend in fatal crashes has been favourable, decreasing from 397 in

2005, to 365 in 2006, to 339 in 2007. In 2009, the European Road Safety Performance Index programme, which is run by the European Transport Safety Council, ranked Ireland sixth in the top ten best performing EU countries for road safety performance.

The National and European fight against road carnage is working with countries introducing novel ways to curb the problem. Australia introduced 'booze-buses' in 1989, which enabled blood alcohol tests to be done on the spot, producing results that were acceptable in court as evidence. Whole areas were targeted in blitzes and the number of detections fell away quickly as drivers got the message. So there are valuable lessons to be learned from our European neighbours and beyond. Sweden has taken its campaign a step further with the adoption of Vision Zero, a policy that basically states that no amount of serious injuries and road deaths should be tolerated. In general terms, crashes and fatalities on the roads are seen as a necessary evil to be accepted in the interests of personal mobility. Not any more, says Sweden, which is arguably the safest place to drive in Europe. It has always been at the forefront of road safety – being one of the first countries to require seat belts for both front and rear seats.

Vision Zero accepts that crashes will happen, so the best course of action is to try to minimise the effects; for example, traffic is slowed, roads are improved, crash barriers are put up, and rigid roadside objects like overgrown bushes or trees are removed. The Swedish government says that central safety barriers have reduced head-on smashes by 80 per cent, while lowering speed limits in urban areas has reduced injuries to cyclists and pedestrians by 50 per cent. The Vision Zero policy is being copied in countries around the world, including Norway and Australia. Conor Faughnan would love to see it implemented here. 'The only acceptable number of road deaths is zero,' he says.

14

THE LEGAL ROUTE

'There is no level of alcohol in the blood at which driving is safe.'
Dr Declan Bedford

Drink-driving kills an estimated 10,000 people in Europe every year. In Ireland alone, alcohol was a contributory factor in 1,000 deaths between 1999 and 2008. When Sweden reduced its drink-driving limits from 80 mg to 50 mg per 100 ml of blood in 2005, the result was an enormous 44 per cent cut in alcohol-related deaths in just two years. These stark facts speak for themselves, and were top of the agenda at an international road safety conference in Dublin Castle in October 2009. The event, hosted by the Road Safety Authority and attended by European experts, was held to mark the start of Irish Road Safety Week.

The best minds in Europe with regard to road safety joined forces to share vital information and ideas on how to tackle the problem of road carnage. Each of the speakers could relate to what the other was saying because unfortunately, road deaths are not unique to any one country, but common to all. Every expert held the same view on drinking and driving: the two should never go together.

Members of the European Transport Safety Council delivered a number of lectures on drink-driving. The Brussels-based independent organisation is dedicated to reducing the number of road deaths and injuries in Europe. Board Director, Professor Richard Allsop, told the audience, 'If no one drove while impaired by alcohol, an estimated 6,000 lives would have been saved across the EU in 2008 alone'. He continued, 'measures to tackle drink-driving are available, including comprehensive legislative provisions, thorough police enforcement and modern in-car technologies. Focusing on repeat offenders and drivers caught with very high Blood Alcohol Concentration (BAC) is an important first step, but it's not enough by itself. It's also necessary to persuade moderate drinkers to organise their lives so that they do not drive after drinking.'

Transport Minister, Noel Dempsey TD, attended the conference. He took to the stage and said, 'Alcohol may have been a contributory factor in over 1,000 fatal collisions on Irish roads between 1999 and 2008. The reality behind these statistics is lives lost, grieving families and shattered communities. The overwhelming body of scientific evidence could not be any clearer. Any amount of alcohol impairs driving and increases the risk of being in a crash. Thankfully the majority of people in this country now believe that drinking and driving is simply not acceptable behaviour in today's society.'

It might be a widely held belief that such behaviour is no longer socially acceptable, but the problem of drink-driving, though much improved, still persists. According to the Road Safety Authority, 18,851 drivers were arrested on suspicion of drink-driving in 2007, while the figure for 2008 was 18,053. That's an average of around 347 drivers a week arrested on suspicion of being over the limit.

The conference also heard from Dr Declan Bedford, a leading public health expert, who has carried out extensive research on drink-driving. He believes that Ireland has a chronic drink problem, 'Of all the World Health Organisation regions, Europe has the highest consumption of alcohol and, within Europe, Ireland is more or less always at the top of the table. This is compounded by the fact that we binge drink. We concentrate our drinking at the weekend when we see an increase in alcohol-related road crashes.'

Dr Bedford carried out an analysis for the Health Service Executive of 995 crashes between 2003 and 2005 in which more than 1,000 people were killed. He presented his findings to the conference, insisting that there is no level of alcohol in the blood at which driving was safe. He discovered that alcohol was a factor in one in three fatal crashes. He also found that drink-driving is a male problem. 'Ninety per cent of drivers, whose alcohol was a contributory factor in a fatal crash, were men,' he said. 'Driver alcohol was a factor in 62 per cent of single-vehicle, single-occupant fatal crashes. Twenty-one per cent of fatal road crashes that happen between 6 a.m. and 12 noon are alcohol-related, and one in four pedestrians killed had been drinking.'

As shocking as these statistics are, Dr Bedford says they do not accurately reflect the crisis. 'The data I collected from

Garda files is basically an underestimate of the true problem, because when I examined the reports, I discovered that more than a third of the drivers killed were not tested for alcohol and drugs. This is why I believe mandatory alcohol testing after all crashes would be of benefit, as it would highlight the true extent of alcohol in crashes.' His research may be considered instrumental in the arguments for lowering the drink-driving limits in Ireland, and for mandatory alcohol testing at crash scenes. Just three weeks on from the road safety conference in Dublin Castle, Minister Dempsey published the new Road Traffic Bill on 30 October 2009, which included provisions for those exact changes.

The new Road Traffic Bill contains proposals to reduce the BAC for drivers, from 80 mg to 50 mg per 100 ml of blood. This will drop even further for learner drivers and professional drivers – down to 20 mg – less than one drink. Not everyone was ready to welcome the new laws. Up to twenty Fianna Fáil backbenchers vowed to vote against the bill, which they considered too severe. Much of their concern centred on the effect it would have on rural communities. Minister Dempsey responded to this pressure by reducing the proposed penalties for drivers caught under the new, lower drink-drive limits. He had previously indicated that drivers caught with a blood alcohol level of between 50 mg and 80 mg would receive six penalty points and a fine. Now, the legislation states that those drivers will instead face three penalty points and a €200 fine if they do not challenge the conviction in court. It is the first time the State has had a penalty for drink-driving that does not include a driving ban.

Drivers with a blood alcohol concentration of between

80 mg and 100 mg will be disqualified for six months and receive a €400 fine, if they do not challenge the conviction. Learners, recently qualified and professional drivers found to have a blood alcohol concentration of between 20 mg and 80 mg will be disqualified for three months and receive a €200 fine. In the event of a court appearance and conviction, drivers found with BACs of less than 80 mg will be disqualified for six months for a first offence and for one year on any subsequent offence. The legislation provides for penalty points and disqualifications to be applied to non-national driving licences. It also allows for mandatory alcohol testing of drivers involved in crashes and the introduction of impairment testing of drivers.

Minister Dempsey says, 'The aim of the bill is to improve road safety and save lives and reduce serious injuries on our roads. Intoxicated driving is one of the main causes of deaths and injuries on our roads and that is no longer acceptable. The research in this area is conclusive and irrefutable. I know that this will save lives. It's the right thing to do.'

Dr Declan Bedford welcomes the bill. He says that even one drink can impair driving significantly. 'Evidence shows that driving becomes impaired after very low levels of alcohol consumption. A driver becomes seriously impaired at about 50 mg. If you ask an average person how much they can drink to be under 80 mg, you will get a variety of answers. Lowering the limits means there's less confusion. Rather than thinking, "I can get away with two or three pints", people will think, "it's getting so low, I don't think I can drink and drive at all".' He is confident that the government will vote for the new Road Traffic Bill. 'I think it will pass without much opposition. Noel Dempsey is showing leadership. He is also being pragmatic in lowering the penalties in order to keep his backbenchers happy. We can't afford to stay behind Europe on this issue. Of course, I would prefer to see a ban for everyone caught drinking and driving rather than just three penalty points for a first offence. At least the punishment for a second offence in the 50 to 80 mg range is a ban from driving. I think this legislation will completely change the culture of drinking and driving.'

Minister Noel Dempsey admits he has concerns about the amount of time it takes to implement changes in politics. He may not like it, but he will have a long wait for his Road Traffic Bill to be enforced. Following the publication of the bill, it was confirmed that ten-year-old equipment used to test breath samples will have to be replaced to incorporate the new drink-driving limits. Professor Denis Cusack of the Medical Bureau of Road Safety, which provides and monitors the equipment, explains, 'There are currently sixty-four breath-testing machines in Garda stations around the country but these cannot be recalibrated to the new limits proposed in the Road Traffic Bill 2009. This will push back the introduction of the law until 2011.' He explains that some handheld machines used at the roadside can be recalibrated effectively, but many more devices are needed. The bill also has to be passed in both houses of the Oireactas and become law, before the new devices can be purchased, in case of any last minute changes.

Minister Dempsey said he was not worried about the possible effect of the changes on rural Ireland. 'I'm not concerned. If rural Ireland is dependent on us allowing people to get into a car with an excess of alcohol in their blood, put themselves or other road users in danger, then rural Ireland has come to a sorry state. I don't believe it's in that state. I believe that the issue of rural isolation is one that can be addressed. It will be an adjustment for some, but many already take on board the implications of alcohol and are not drinking and driving. Crashes, deaths and injuries on our roads and their traumatic effects on families and communities are also social issues in both rural and urban areas.'

Likewise, Dr Declan Bedford believes the rural isolation argument is overstated. 'There were no submissions made to the Road Safety Authority by rural associations like the Irish Country Women's Association and Macra Na Feirme. In fact, Macra na Feirme came out in support of the bill. I think we have an over-dependence on alcohol. I hear publicans and politicians talk about men who come down to the pub to play cards midweek and have one drink. Well, why can't that one drink be tea or a soft drink? They could still get to play cards. That's the social element anyway. Or they could share the driving; take turns to drive each other home.'

One of the most vocal opponents of the bill is Independent Kerry South TD Jackie Healy Rae, who has said that he will not be voting with the government on this issue for the first time in twelve years. He has been quoted in the *Irish Independent* as saying, 'Alcohol has nothing whatsoever to do with the number of people being killed on our roads. The longer the bill is kept at bay, the more I'll like it.' His remarks reflect the equally controversial opinions of Fianna Fáil backbencher Mattie McGrath, who has said that one drink could relax nervous drivers.

The World Health Organisation holds a different view. Its 'Global Status Report on Road Safety' (WHO 2009), states that the risk of involvement in a crash increases significantly if a driver's blood alcohol level is above 40 mg. It found that laws which establish lower BACs for novice drivers (between zero and 20 mg) can lead to reductions of between 4 and 24 per cent in the number of crashes involving young people. It suggests that drink-driving laws should be based on blood alcohol concentration of 50 mg or below, and recommends that all countries should set limits of 20 mg or below for young drivers. The United Kingdom and Malta are the only two other European countries with higher BACs of 80 mg and 90 mg respectively.

CONCLUSION

My first car, a second-hand navy-blue Ford Fiesta, leaked oil like a running tap. A work colleague drove me out to the small country garage outside Athlone to seal the deal. The exchange happened, one cheque for one key. 'Wait for me,' I urged my friend, who was already well experienced in the art of driving; 'let me follow you.' He smiled, telling me to relax. But I couldn't relax, because I was afraid I would forget which foot went where. 'Accelerator, brake, clutch,' I told myself, 'It's as easy as ABC.' Then I ventured out onto the main Dublin to Galway road, the artery from east to west, my eyes locked on the square boot of my colleague's car in front. My first provisional licence was tucked into the glove compartment.

The year was 1997 and my dismal road safety record was about to get worse. My youngest brother had taught me how to drive since no one else had the patience. My father's car bore the brunt of those lessons, scrapes, dents and a bruised bumper. *Titanic*, one of the most expensive movies ever made, was definitely the most expensive movie I ever saw.

The evening cost me £500 in total, the amount required to repair the car I dented while trying to park – ironically, the car belonged to County Offaly's Road Safety Officer.

I moved from the Midlands back to the Big Smoke. I had left Dublin as a pedestrian, and was now returning as a driver, albeit not a very good one. From the start, things did not run smoothly. I was on first-name terms with city-centre clampers, and the collection of yellow-and-black parking tickets stuffed along my dashboard reminded me of a swarm of bees. Every time I looked at them, I felt a sting. My traffic violations came to a head one morning in Pearse Street near Trinity College. I was driving in a bus lane, with a broken seat belt while talking on my brick-sized mobile phone. A young garda on a motorbike pulled up alongside me. When he asked me what I was driving in and I responded 'traffic', he was unimpressed. But at the time, he could not penalise me for talking on the phone: that only became an offence on 16 July 2006.

Thankfully, my driving has improved immensely over the last decade, and that is down to experience. I sold my navy-blue Fiesta and never looked back. The genuine fear I felt that first day when pulling out of the forecourt has disappeared, but in different ways I know the road is still as threatening as ever. I respect it now, rather than fear it. My attitude has matured; but it is only since writing this book that my behaviour as a road user changed dramatically for the better.

Cars are still costing me too much money. My friend described my old scarlet Opel Corsa as a 'crap-box'. Eventually, he wore me down and, in summer 2007, I splashed out on a brand new Mini. My fresh set of wheels caused me to drive with extreme caution, mainly because I was afraid of marking the shiny car in any way. But I still took unnecessary risks, clocking up speed on motorways, and getting caught for my haste. On one occasion, I was rushing to catch a plane at Shannon. The garda did not care, and rightly so. My four penalty points did act as a deterrent: I slowed down. However, it was not until I met those I spoke to while researching this book that I began sticking to the speed limits everywhere. I stopped overtaking so much. I finally realised the fatal consequences of rushing on the roads. I didn't want to be 'dead on time'. Their stories changed how I drive and my express hope is that they may also change the way we all drive.

I remember the first day I was introduced to some of the courageous families who were kind enough to contribute to this book. It was the Friday before Christmas 2008. A group of people had gathered in the festive grounds of Farmleigh House in Dublin's Phoenix Park. An outdoor crib overlooked the manicured lawns. Inside, a 12-foot-high tree with white fairy lights dominated the function room. None of these people wanted to be there. They were present only because of what they had in common: a shared grief, the loss of a loved one on Irish roads. As I glanced around the room, I wondered what it would feel like to have an empty place always at the Christmas dinner table; to be part of a splintered family.

Beneath the high ceilings and sparkling chandeliers, everyone took their seats. The lights dimmed for the screening of the Road Safety Authority's new television advertising campaign, featuring true-life road tragedies. The series, called 'Crashed Lives', consists of heartbreaking stories, told by bereaved families. Each speaks about the loss of a loved one in a road collision and how it has changed their lives for ever. They open their hearts and the rawness of their grief to the nation, so that others can see what it is like to lose someone close on the roads. That morning, they came as invited guests to Farmleigh; this was their premiere.

The audience was quiet, stunned into silence. Fighting back tears, I could have a heard a pin drop. A heavy sadness hung in the room, as journalists, photographers, gardaí, paramedics and families watched and listened. It was harder somehow to see this screening with the stars of the adverts in the same room. People brought hands to their mouths, placed fingers on lips, averted their eyes from the huge screen, but there was no escaping the harsh reality of what was being shown. RTÉ's Miriam O'Callaghan performed the official launch. She thanked the families for their contributions to road safety. 'Ireland owes you a debt,' she said.

The legacy of these families is one that should never be forgotten. Their stories help to save lives. I met with them afterwards, when the lights came up, and some agreed to tell me more about their lives than what they had summed up in the fifty-second adverts. The idea for this book had already taken shape in my mind. Meeting these brave people, who have suffered unbearable grief, inspired me to turn the thought into a concrete plan.

Through the course of my research, I have met many others who have suffered as a direct result of road crashes, each with their own tragic tales. One bereaved father told me that when he hears the news of a fatal crash on a Monday morning, he feels sickened. 'It is somebody else's turn this weekend,' he says. 'When will it all stop?' For him, and so many others like him, the pain of grief will never go away, but they still cling to the hope that the roads will become a safer place. I am astounded still at the kindness shown to me: the open conversations, the shared tears over cups of tea, the photographs admired, and the searing pain in so many eyes, all wishing they could turn back the clock. The people featured in this book cannot change the past. But, they just might be able – if people will listen – to change the future.

ACKNOWLEDGEMENTS

This book would not have been possible without the many bereaved and injured people who shared their stories with such brutal honesty and open hearts: to them, most of all, I am forever grateful. I would also like to thank my family, Mam, Dad, Nick, Andy and Jane, Granny and Tom, Moya for her unbelievable genorisity at all times with everything, Treena for the space to write, Rose for reading the odd chapter, and all my extended family for their support.

I researched this subject for a few months. Those working on the front line encounter tragedy as part of their daily lives, and I am grateful that they took the time to explain how difficult that can be. I would like to thank everyone I interviewed for this book, those included among the pages and those behind the scenes. This project took shape during my MA in Writing at NUIG. I would like to thank Dr Adrian Frazier and Jonathan Williams for their encouragement and advice, as well as my fellow writers. TV3's Bob Hughes and Andrew Hanlon allowed me the time to complete the course, and I am extremely grateful to them. Susan Millar DuMars and Kevin Higgins got me writing in the first place, thanks, guys. To Michael for all his encouragement and support from the beginning. I would like to thank The Collins Press for believing in this project. From day one, the Road Safety Authority was very supportive and I thank Noel Brett, Gay Byrne and the staff.

Finally to my colleagues and friends, Helen and Emma in particular, and anyone I may have unwittingly failed to mention, thanks for everything.